Middleton in *Emmerdale Farm* for a short time. Since then, I have seen Dinah at a party given to celebrate the 501st episode of *This is Your Life*. It was also her seventieth birthday, so we were all very pleased to sing 'Happy Birthday'.

Andrew Sachs also appeared on my *This is Your Life*. I had first worked with him in rep in Bexhill, then he joined Brian's company in *Simple Spymen* at the Whitehall Theatre. What a funny man he is, and so clever.

Next was a lovely, farcical film called *Under Beds, Behind Doors*, which Irene Handl, Derek Royle, Bob Todd, Nicholas Parsons and 'Slim' Ramsden had put together. It was hysterically funny and sometimes, if I'm feeling in the dumps, I play it and laugh again. All of them had worked with me at some time or another during my years with Brian and the Whitehall Theatre crowd.

The film started with Irene—who was in the film *The Night We Got the Bird* with me—stepping into a wardrobe with a parrot. Various shenanigans followed, in true Whitehall style, and it all ended with Bob Todd saluting me, his trousers promptly falling down. Bob had been in

the stage run of *Chase Me, Comrade!*, as had Derek, who took over from Larry Noble during its last months.

Bob is an example of someone who came to showbusiness late, in his case after spending many years as a farmer. At the age of forty-two, he became an actor and stooged to some of the great television comedians, such as Sid James in *Citizen James*, Dick Emery in his shows and Marty Feldman in *Marty*, before teaming up with Benny Hill.

Derek Royle was part of a showbusiness family, with his daughters Carol and Amanda carrying on the acting tradition. Sadly, he and the other stars of that dear little film are also no longer with us, apart from Nicholas Parsons, who starred in my last West End farce, *Uproar in the House*, and 'Slim' Ramsden, who had been in *Chase Me, Comrade!* at the Whitehall and Brian's repertoire at the Garrick.

Then, my darling Frazer Hines came on. He was taking a break from *Emmerdale Farm* at the time and touring in a play. It was so good to see him—he's quite my favourite person after my family.

Nicholas Parsons walked on with a custard pie all over his face—from that

filmed piece earlier. Better love hath no man than this, that he gets a custard pie in his face. He was terribly funny and kept making mistakes and correcting them. Nicholas is, of course, known as presenter of *Sale of the Century,* but he's always been an actor in films and theatre, and is a great pro to work with—always on the ball—and will help you out when necessary.

Rosalind Iden came on. Now there's a name from the past. She was, of course, Sir Donald Wolfit's wife, Lady Wolfit, and I had toured with her at the beginning of the war. She was clearly very much in love with Donald then and we were so glad to hear that she eventually married him.

She was, in fact, his third wife and has an interesting story of her own. She was the daughter of Ben Iden Payne, who had persuaded Miss A. E. F. Horniman, the tea heiress, to lease the Gaiety Theatre in Manchester so that he could start the first repertory company in England. It was while he and his actress wife Mona Limerick were there, in 1911, that their daughter was born.

She studied as a ballerina and became ballet mistress at the Old Vic Theatre, but forewent the opportunity to create the

Sadler's Wells Ballet Company, presented to her by Lilian Baylis, who took a close interest in her career.

It was the need to earn more money that led Rosalind into acting and she was given a boost by her father, who cast her in a season at the Stratford Memorial Theatre after becoming director there. Donald then engaged her in his company and later she became his leading lady both on stage and off.

The last arrival for my *This is Your Life* was my precious grandson, David, who came on with his mother, Rosina. He came towards us with a posy of flowers and, as he offered it to me, Eamonn pushed the big red book into my hands, so I wasn't able to pick up the posy. I was so upset, but it all ended with a lovely party and everybody let their hair down.

I was slightly disappointed, and surprised, that a great friend of mine, Helen Jessop—who now lives and works in Johannesburg—had not been flown in. Apparently, she was asked, but her theatre boss wouldn't release her. What a shame. Also, my chum Anna Dawson had not been able to make it.

But the show was a wonderful experience

and I'm so glad Peter lied to me. 'I can get away with anything with you now,' he said afterwards. 'I've been lying to you for the past few months.' It must have been very difficult for him.

Getting selected for an appearance on *This is Your Life* is just one of the signs that you have made it in showbusiness. Fame and fan letters are something to which I soon became accustomed when *Emmerdale Farm* turned out to be so popular.

People often ask me if I am as good a cook as Annie. Well, I hope so. I won't say that I like cooking, because it takes up so much time, but I do get a buzz from seeing people enjoying what I have cooked and leaving an empty plate. I can remember as a child baking my first cake, a Madeira. It was a magnificent success and my father said it was the best cake he had ever tasted.

My next effort was a ground rice cake, but I mistook the ingredients and used semolina. That was a fiasco, a solid piece of wood. But I was allowed to cook steak at home. Although we had two maids, their idea of cooking steak was to put it in the oven and it came out like charcoal, so I was given the honours.

My favourite meal of all is roast beef, Yorkshire puddings, roast and mashed potatoes, swede, cauliflower cheese, peas and horseradish sauce. Put a plate of that in front of me and it beats all the fancy foreign dishes you can think of.

That's the only similarity between my cooking and that of Annie Sugden, though. She does roast beef and steaks, but I also do many other dishes. If I'm having friends round for dinner, one of my favourites is dressed crab, wrapped up in smoked salmon. That's lovely! Another speciality of mine is fish pie with halibut, salmon and prawns, topped with white sauce and cheese. You're supposed to have that with potatoes, but I'm constantly watching my weight, so I prepare it without. Annie bakes a lot of cakes, which I don't because if you bake them you eat them.

These days, I'm more inclined to take people out if they're coming for dinner. Where I live, there are several good restaurants—an Italian one on the front overlooking the sea, a Chinese takeaway and an Indian where I eat when my son, Nigel, comes over, but not otherwise.

The success of *Emmerdale* has meant giving interviews to the press and seeing

a plethora of books and special magazines to celebrate the programme's various landmarks, as well as an official monthly *Emmerdale Magazine* launched a couple of years ago. Something I'm always asked for is my favourite recipe. I get fed up of writing down recipes! But I would get worried if such requests stopped.

Fame is one thing, but I cannot bear being grabbed. It's the physical contact to which I object, people grabbing and kissing me. I've had some peculiar letters, too. One man wrote saying, 'You have a beautiful bosom. Will you not wear your apron and draw your hand round the top of your dress, and I shall know you are thinking of me.' I've had quite a few letters of that type!

Inevitably, when starring in television programmes, actors get asked to open jumble sales, shops and all sorts of other things. During the early days of *Emmerdale Farm,* I did many personal appearances. I opened a fête at Arncliffe, where we used to record location shots for the serial, and I was asked back to Hornsea, which was an easy one to do because I was able to talk about my childhood there. In a coal-mining village, I was given the present

of a little Davy-lamp, and other members of the cast would go to bingo halls and give out prizes.

I did personal appearances for about eight years, but I hated them so much—they were such a distraction from the job of making a television programme—that I gave them up. People still ask, but I always say no. If I say yes to one, then I would really have to do them all. Almost all those I used to do were charity events, so I gave my time free. Stars nowadays seem to make a handsome profit out of such appearances.

10
And Then it was Emmerdale

So much has happened to *Emmerdale Farm* on and off screen over the past ten years or so. Already things were changing at the end of our first decade, but we could not have foreseen the almost total transformation that would occur as we carried on through the eighties and into the nineties. Anne Gibbons took over as producer from Michael Glynn and introduced the Merricks and bumptious Alan Turner, who now presides over The Woolpack. He had started his life in Beckindale as manager for NY Estates of the land it had bought in the village and soon became embroiled in rows with the Sugdens over farming.

Caroline Bates arrived with her children, Kathy and Nick. She was separated and later divorced from her husband and Kathy was to fall for Joe Sugden's cousin, Jackie Merrick, whom she eventually married. There was no happy ending as he was

killed in a shooting accident, although the poor girl was later to marry again.

Malandra Burrows, who plays Kathy, is still with us today. She had been on the children's talent show *Junior Showtime* at the age of six and won the New Faces programme three years later—under the stage name Malandra Newman—before training at a drama school in her native Liverpool. After small roles in *The Practice* and *Brookside,* she joined *Emmerdale Farm* and is now one of the programme's longest-serving cast members. She even had a hit single with a song called 'Just This Side of Love', which she performed in the programme.

Diana Davies has been in and out of the show as Malandra's screen mother and had previous experience in soap with *Coronation Street,* playing corner shop assistant Norma Ford, one of Ken Barlow's many girlfriends. She had also been in *Emmerdale Farm* as another character, Letty Brewer, which is something that often happens in long-running TV serials—someone plays a small part and is asked back later to take a more prominent role.

Clive Hornby, who had taken over the

role of Jack Sugden, settled in quickly. He was even honoured with a special dinner at the Queens Hotel in Leeds on his arrival. It was, after all, a very important part that he was coming to play, although his character returned as a completely different person, more dedicated to farming than ever before!

On screen, Jack married Pat Merrick, who had been his childhood sweetheart but went on to marry Tom Merrick. The couple had split up and Pat returned to Beckindale, only to fall for Jack again. It was then that Jack found out he was the father of Pat's son Jackie, born shortly after the pair had broken up. She also had a daughter, Sandie, an auctioneer at nearby Hotten Market, who was also something of a sex siren.

The couple married off screen, too, and actress Helen Weir, who played Pat, eventually left the programme after having a baby, Thomas, so that she could spend time with him. For a year after that, Clive remained in the programme and was very difficult with everyone. He then left, returned later, was a different person and became one of the lynchpins of the serial. Clive and Helen have both remained

good friends and I often stay with them at their beautiful Georgian farmhouse in the Yorkshire Moors at Ilkley while recording the programme in Leeds. In recent years, Clive has taken up golf and even won cups for it.

Frazer Hines, who plays my other screen son, Joe, has been a close friend since the start of the programme, although he left for a while in an attempt to save his marriage to actress Gemma Craven. Unfortunately, they eventually split up and Frazer returned to us less than two years later for a short run, before coming back permanently the following year.

During his time away, he was kept busy with stage work, including a role in *Duty Free* in Cambridge, a season at the prestigious Pitlochry Festival Theatre and a tour of *Doctor in the House*. He also took nine months off to race as an amateur jockey, being an avid horse owner and breeder. Frazer often spoke to me about his troubles and treated me as he would his real mother. All he really wanted was a shoulder to cry on.

The marriage had never really gelled and he was very upset about the whole situation. It was not helped by Frazer and

Gemma being apart for much of the first year. He was in Yorkshire working on *Emmerdale* while she was away, first filming and then starring in the hit stage musical *Song and Dance* in London's West End. Frazer desperately wanted the marriage to work out, but it was not to be and he occupied his mind with his interest in horse racing. Then, a couple of years ago, the whole cast was really pleased for Frazer when he married again.

Frazer's character was not so lucky with his second marriage, to divorcée Kate Hughes. She spent a year in jail for causing death by reckless driving after knocking over Pete Whiteley, who had been having an affair with her daughter, Rachel, and then looked for a new future without Joe. By the time Frazer had come through his own personal troubles and returned to the programme, in the mid-eighties, it was gaining more continuity. Anne Gibbons, our producer, increased the size of the cast and opted for longer-running storylines involving the regulars, rather than bringing in new characters for a short time.

In 1988, it came as something of a shock when Stuart Doughty arrived to

take over the programme after producing the Channel Four serial *Brookside* since its inception. That was very much a 'modern' soap, featuring unemployment, teenage sex and bad language—although the swearing stopped quickly, as viewers switched off in their droves. He left *Brookside* on the crest of a wave, having established it as Channel Four's most popular programme.

Stuart made it clear that he did not intend to turn *Emmerdale Farm* into a rural *Brookside*. But the programme had already become more raunchy—one of the reasons Kevin Laffan, the creator, stopped writing for it—and Stuart took it further down that road, with half-a-dozen major characters written out or choosing to go in the process. He was certainly put through the mill because he had made so many changes. At first, those of us who were left were very upset and there was a lot of bad feeling. Eventually, though, we realised that Stuart was really a nice man at heart.

Beloved friends left and new people took their place, and suddenly *Emmerdale* no longer had 'farm' as part of its title—which was right because much of the action began to take place away from the farm. So it was

like the end of an era, but we soon became used to the new bods and enfolded them in our bosoms.

In 1989, we left the Yorkshire Television studios, which had become home to us, and went to an old mill a few miles out of Leeds that had been converted into studios specially for *Emmerdale*. The move wasn't very popular with me, though, because it added twenty minutes to my journey to work each morning. Also, the mill has an antiquated lift in which I became stuck once and have since refused to travel alone. People are very kind and take me up and down as required. It's either that or walking up three flights of a stone staircase to the rehearsal and dressing-rooms.

Once we had acclimatised ourselves to the new studios, we were again like one big, happy family. This was largely thanks to the caring Tim Fee, who never lost his rag and smoothed the way for whatever tormented us. He used to be our unit manager and is now production supervisor, in charge of the studios. Make a complaint and Tim will put the matter right if it is in his power. He has such a sunny disposition that it rubs off on everyone.

Gradually, the stalwarts of the cast have

223

left. Hugh Manning, who had played the Rev Donald Hinton since the late seventies—and in the previous decade had starred as Hunter with Kathleen Harrison in the hit TV series *Mrs Thursday*—was the first to go and has been sadly missed. Unfortunately, Hugh had not been well since having a hip operation and, during his last few years in *Emmerdale*, he appeared less frequently.

He has had to have another operation since leaving the programme and could walk only with the aid of a stick. It is a shame because he made a marvellous vicar and was very believable in the role. Hugh was once a president of Equity, the actors' union, so he was quite a big noise in the theatre and it really was an honour to have him in the programme.

Next to go was my darling Freddie Pyne, who had been fed up in the role of Matt Skilbeck for a long time and decided to return to the theatre. I miss Freddie dreadfully—he was always a help in times of trouble. I even went on holiday with him to Tenerife once. He was so patient and caring, putting up with an old woman who couldn't easily get up and down stairs. In fact, Playa de las Americas is full of

steps, so it was difficult to go anywhere without negotiating them. We had a lovely week lying in the sun, doing absolutely nothing, which was what we both needed after months of working in the studios.

Freddie was such a kind person. When I stopped driving up to Leeds every week, he would take me in his old Humber. He lived in Streatham, South London, and I used to meet him outside Waterloo station.

Peter Alexander had played builder Phil Pearce for only three years, but was the first cast member to get the chop after Stuart Doughty's arrival, with his character being despatched to prison. Peter himself knew something about farming, having his own smallholding in the Pennines. It is very beautiful and he has lambs there. These days, he directs pantomimes and popped up on TV a couple of years ago in episodes of the comedy series *Singles* and the nostalgic drama *Heartbeat*, which are both made by Yorkshire Television. He has also made guest appearances in *Coronation Street* and *Brookside*.

Another of the younger members of the cast to go was Ian Sharrock, who played Jackie Merrick. The character was killed in a shooting accident and Ian—who had

met wife Pam when she was working as a secretary in the press office at Yorkshire Television—has since returned to Leeds on stage in *Wild Oats*, the opening production at the new West Yorkshire Playhouse. As a child actor, he had appeared in the TV musical *Smike* and, later, in the controversial television play *Scum*, as well as the film *Candleshoe*.

When Ronnie Magill decided to leave after a period of feeling unsettled, another pillar was knocked down. He played the role of Amos Brearly with great gusto and was another original member of the cast. Before joining the programme, he had been highly respected in the theatre world, spending nine years as actor and artistic director at the Nottingham Playhouse, where he worked with directors such as the legendary Tyrone Guthrie.

He was certainly fêted when he left us, earning a Variety Club of Great Britain luncheon in his honour. He also had a party with all the cast, and Cy Chadwick—who plays Nick Bates—turned director to make a video for him, with a script by Tony Pitts (Archie Brooks) in which I acted a drunken Annie, complete with a plate of Campari scones.

Many of the cast played members of the production team, with Tony Pitts memorably acting Stuart Doughty. Ronnie then appeared on Terry Wogan's chat-show, where he had his famous side-burns ceremoniously shaved off.

In his last episode of *Emmerdale*, I found the farewell outside The Woolpack between two old friends—Amos and Henry Wilks—very moving. Of course, Ronnie made a couple of brief returns to whisk Annie off to Spain on long holidays, when I took three-month winter breaks from the programme. I was no longer able to make the journey to Leeds on those icy mornings.

I was also sorry to see Jean Rogers leave the cast. She had taken over the role of Dolly Skilbeck in 1980 and, eleven years later, was written out. Jean had been a good friend, another who was always there in times of trouble.

She once drove me back to our Leeds house when a message arrived at the Yorkshire Television studios that Peter had been taken ill with an asthma attack and couldn't breathe. I phoned the doctor, who said I should get back pretty damn quick, and Jean rushed me home in her car. When

we arrived, the doctor and ambulance were there and Peter looked dreadful.

He was whisked off to hospital—St James's in Leeds, more recently featured in *Jimmy's*, the real-life hospital series—and given all sorts of emergency treatments, before being put to bed in a room of his own. We were told there was nothing more I could do, so Jean and I went back to work.

I visited Peter that evening and every time I could find a spare minute. One morning, he felt terrible and told me, 'I don't want to die.' I said that of course he wouldn't die but he had to have patience. Then I phoned the charge nurse to tell him what Peter had said to me and asked him to speak to Peter and reassure him, which he did, making him feel much better. I must admit, there were times when I thought Peter wouldn't pull through, but the nursing staff at St James's are second to none and he was home in about ten days.

He occasionally had bad attacks after that, but then bought a nebuliser, which went everywhere with him. It was incredible how quickly he could control it with the help of antibiotics and steroids. He still

had to be careful, though, and at the first sign of a cough or cold took his steroids and used the nebuliser.

When she left, Jean made it clear she was unhappy with the way the scriptwriters had dealt with her character's fling with nasty Charlie Aindow and her subsequent abortion. She was obviously upset about being axed from the cast, though. Since Freddie Pyne had gone as her screen husband, I think the scriptwriters were constantly having to find storylines for Jean.

Jean is such a professional that she will always work. Before joining *Emmerdale*, she was already well known for her roles as Nurse Rogers in *Emergency—Ward 10* and Julie Shepherd in *Crossroads*, and had made numerous other TV appearances, as well as acting in and presenting radio programmes such as *Listen with Mother* and *Children's Hour*.

I still see Jean occasionally when she's performing on stage near me. A couple of years before leaving the programme, she married Phil Hartley, who had been a floor manager on the programme. Both had been married before and, between them, the couple have six children.

But the greatest blow to hit us on *Emmerdale* since the death of Toke Townley was the news that Arthur Pentelow had died. He had played Henry Wilks since the programme began, for almost all that time as joint owner of The Woolpack, forming a memorable double-act alongside Ronnie Magill as Amos. Henry was also a director of Emmerdale Farm—when it became a limited company in the early episodes of the serial—a good friend of Annie's and someone whose advice she respected.

Much the same can be said of Arthur and me. He was a great friend and I was devastated when I heard of his death. Apparently, he had been driving back to Leeds from his family home in Birmingham when he suffered a heart attack at the wheel of his car. Arthur was within a mile of his house near Leeds and the police found him slumped over the steering wheel, with the engine still running. The awful thing was that he was alone and so close to home.

The most charming man, whom everybody loved, Arthur never had a bad word to say about anyone and no one said a bad word about him. He was also very generous, always willing to put his hand in his pocket to help people out.

As an actor, he was totally professional but, when the working week was over, he would go straight back home to his wife, Jacqueline.

Arthur was another of those who went into acting late. He started his career as a cadet clerk in the police force in his native Rochdale, before serving in the Navy during the Second World War. Afterwards, he became a student teacher, but his love of acting—which went back to his schooldays, when he studied Shakespeare—led him to join the then new Bradford Civic Playhouse Theatre School, under the tuition of Esmé Church.

Later, he appeared on stage in Orson Welles's acclaimed London West End production of *Othello*, in films such as *Charlie Bubbles* and *Privilege*, and in many television programmes. He had already appeared in *Compact*, the serial about a women's magazine, and as the football supporters' club chairman in *United!* when he landed the role of park-keeper George Greenwood in *Coronation Street*, the character being an old friend of Hilda Ogden who gave Emily Bishop driving lessons.

Arthur, of course, was in *Emmerdale* right

from the start. As Henry, he asked Annie to marry him more than once. There was one story I especially remember, when Annie was on a valium trip after being prescribed the drug for some illness or another. Henry threw the tablets away and there was a terrible scene, with Annie screaming at him for doing so and Henry calling the doctor. Annie subsequently suffered withdrawal symptoms when she was taken off the valium. The whole thing was so real because I take valium myself to sleep, but not all day long, as Annie did, and wondered what would ever happen if I stopped taking the tablets.

As with Toke's death, the passing of Arthur marked for me a watershed in life on and off screen. Like Toke, I not only loved him but could count him as another surviving member of the original cast. Now, there are only Frazer Hines and myself.

We moved on to another producer, Morag Bain, and in the story the Tates and their Holiday Village began to assume more importance than the faithful old Sugdens, who had to sell the old stone farm-house that had been in their family for three generations because of subsidence, after it

was discovered that the house had been built on an old mine. Jack and Sarah bought neighbouring Hawthorn Cottage and later renamed it Emmerdale.

This momentous event—only the first of several—occurred in 1993, the year in which *Emmerdale* celebrated its twenty-first anniversary. As well as fitting in with the change of emphasis in the programme, this storyline was the result of the real-life farm we used for outdoor shots no longer being worked, following the retirement of Arthur Bell, the tenant farmer there.

His farm, in the village of Lindley, near Otley, had been used in the serial since the first episode. For many years, viewers had seen the sun setting over Emmerdale Farm in the title sequence, but even that had changed by the time the cast were ready to start their anniversary celebrations. Tony Hatch's theme music, too, had been given a revamp as part of an attempt to attract more younger viewers.

The cast was certainly getting much younger. I have done a lot of scenes with Glenda and Craig McKay, who were brought in to play Joe's stepchildren, Rachel and Mark Hughes—the only real-life brother and sister to play the same

roles on screen—when Stuart Doughty took over as producer and gave the programme a revamp.

They were both at school at the time of their début in *Emmerdale*, although Glenda had already taken the role of Gudrun in Ken Russell's film version of *The Rainbow*, the D. H. Lawrence classic. Ironically, Glenda's mother had named her after the actress Glenda Jackson, who had played the grown-up Gudrun in Russell's film of *Women in Love* and acted that character's mother in *The Rainbow* (yes, it might be confusing, but they were filmed that way round). Craig had appeared in two other Yorkshire Television programmes, *The Book Tower* and *How We Used to Live*, while taking his GCSEs.

Other young characters arrived, too, such as Zoe Tate, daughter of Frank and Kim Tate, who bought Home Farm, which they eventually turned into the Holiday Village. Leah Bracknell, who plays Zoe, is the daughter of the late David Bracknell, an assistant film director, and had appeared in programmes such as *The Cannon & Ball Show* and *The Bill* before joining *Emmerdale*. She took a break from the programme to have a baby daughter, Lily,

but returned full-time and soon had a controversial storyline with the revelation that her character was a lesbian—something with which her screen father and brother found difficult to cope.

Her father, of course, is played by Norman Bowler, famous for his role as Det Chief Insp Harry Hawkins in *Softly Softly*, which he played for eleven years. Later, he joined *Crossroads* as a newspaper editor, Sam Benson, so he was used to developing characters on television. He has certainly been allowed to do that in *Emmerdale*, with Frank Tate becoming probably the most important person in Beckindale—certainly the most powerful, despite his business and marriage problems.

Claire King, who plays his screen wife Kim, is always in the newspapers, usually talking about her lively past. She once sang in a punk group and appeared in promotional videos for other acts such as Elvis Costello and Zodiac Mindwarp, whose lead singer, Geoff Bird, she lived with for a while. Claire also acted on television in *Hot Metal* and *The Bill*, and presented an American pop programme called *Shout*.

When Nicholas Prosser took over as

producer in 1993, two Southern families were introduced, with the aim of attracting more viewers in that part of the country. First in were the Windsor family, with the father, Vic—something of a wide boy—being played by Alun Lewis. He was best known up to then as Daryl (Tracey's imprisoned husband) in the comedy series *Birds of a Feather*, although he had previously appeared in *Emmerdale* as a character called Tony Barclay. Alun himself had moved up to Yorkshire from London five years earlier, so his character was following in his own footsteps.

The Windsors took over the village post office in Beckindale, which had not previously been seen in the programme. Yorkshire Television even went on location filming in London when Vic's stepson Scott ran away in the story. This was a complex operation that involved getting thirty technical staff, plus cameras, costumes and props, from Leeds to London. Then along came the new village doctor, Bernard McAllister, and his family, giving a bit of a yuppie flavour to the community.

As you can see, a lot has changed in *Emmerdale*, but Annie is still there, marching on into old age and oblivious

to some of the steamy goings-on around her. Of course, life took another direction for her after she decided to marry again, although that was short-lived as a result of the cataclysmic event that stunned viewers and cast alike—the plane crash over Beckindale that killed off more of the actors. With that, *Emmerdale* entered another phase, at the same time as my own life was to undergo great turmoil.

11
My Leading Man

I have written very little about Peter, my beloved husband. He was a man with great charisma and I was always proud to be his wife. His stage career started when he trained at the Webber Douglas Academy of Dramatic Art after leaving the Fleet Air Arm. Because he was so good-looking, he never wanted for work and spent years playing leading parts in repertory theatre.

One of his favourite roles was Stanley in *A Streetcar Named Desire,* a wonderful play that won Tennessee Williams his first Pulitzer Prize. Peter gave a superb performance in that. Then, in 1952, he joined my brother Brian at the Whitehall Theatre and stayed with him as a stage director and actor, eventually playing parts in *Dry Rot, Simple Spymen* and *One for the Pot.*

When he lost his nerve in the theatre, he decided not to go into Brian's next play and the two of us went into that disastrous venture taking over a pub. He made a

239

wonderful landlord, though, because he could always make people laugh, myself included, which was one of the things about him that I loved.

After leaving the pub, he stayed with Donald Albery as relief front-of-house manager for eighteen months, until Ray Cooney asked him to become his general manager. He helped to put on so many successes for Ray, but the pace was too much for him and he had a nervous breakdown.

On coming up to Leeds, where I was working during the week, he sold products for Niagara that helped people with their aches and pains. However, that was a dead-end job and Peter joined a firm selling telephone answer machines, but he didn't really like selling and soon gave that up. Peter drifted for a while, doing nothing in particular.

Unfortunately, he had a late onset of asthma and was very ill for a long time. He heard about a firm in Bognor Regis that sold nebulisers and travelled down to buy one. They are a fantastic aid to asthma sufferers and cured him of an attack many times. It was while talking to the salesman that the word 'hypnotherapy' came up. Peter cottoned on to this and eventually

took a course in Bournemouth, which he passed with flying colours. He studied widely and the local library had plenty of books written by famous psychotherapists.

As a result, Peter opened a practice in Leeds and was an instant success, with many people cured of phobias, skin diseases, sexual problems and smoking, people who had been abused in childhood —so many things. He had letters galore from people saying how wonderful he was. After every successful patient left him, he used to say, 'I can walk on water. They think I'm God.'

One of his first patients was me—he stopped me smoking. It's a habit I began at drama school because they said you must be able to smoke with ease on stage. As it happens, I've never had a cigarette on stage in my whole life, but I became really hooked on them.

I originally stopped smoking when we moved to that awful pub and didn't start again until the second year of *Emmerdale*, when the tension began to get to me. I had my first cigarette with a drink, of course, and was hooked again. So Peter stopped me by putting me into a state of deep relaxation and talking about the awful

things that smoking can do to the body—it's called suggestion and aversion therapy—and I have not had a cigarette since. I won't say I never get the urge. I do, but I know I must never accept even a puff because that's disaster time. Peter himself smoked until he contracted jaundice while we were in rep together in Huddersfield.

Years passed and Peter got itchy feet, deciding he wanted to live by the sea. Although he liked Walmer, in Kent, where we have good friends, I didn't want to live there because you have to travel on too many motorways for my liking. So we sold our home in Shepperton, Middlesex, and in June 1989 moved to Angmering-on-Sea, a short distance from Worthing, in West Sussex. We were next to the sea and had a house with a swimming pool.

I was dreading moving day, but it went unbelievably smoothly. Rosina, Nigel's wife, travelled with us and I went to bed with the place in chaos. When I walked downstairs the next morning, I looked around and all the packing cases had gone. 'Where is everything?' I asked. Rosina had stayed up half the night and put everything away. She really is a daughter-in-law in a million.

the best of the story is yet to come

Peter and I loved our new home. We only had to walk across the road, through the snicket, and there was the beach and the sea. The weather was kinder to us, with hot summers, although the sea was not brilliant for bathing, so the pool was a real bonus. To walk on the grassy area in front of the sea is a joy because there are always so many people with dogs of all varieties. Mind you, you have to watch where you step!

We found we had some super neighbours, all very friendly and helpful. One couple are also dog-lovers, with five bitches, three black Alsatians and two Heinz. One of the Alsatians appears very fierce and flings himself at the door and barks whenever anyone passes. But, once inside the house, he is told you're a friend and is lovely. I had trouble coping with one dog, but five... Another friend in the area, Moira Butt, used to be in London West End musicals and has three Yorkies, miniatures. They also raise the roof, but are very sweet.

Peter took offices in Littlehampton and was again very successful, but a noisy fast-food shop moved in below, and you cannot practise hypnotherapy with noise.

He therefore worked from home for a while and eventually decided to retire. He was sixty-eight, so it was feasible, and I was seventy-four and still working.

It was clear then that Peter was not in good health, so he spent a lot of time and money having X-rays and excavations. In the end, the doctors carried out a biopsy and found a benign tumour in his bowel. The surgeons said it might turn malignant in around five years so it would be better if he had it operated on and removed now, while he was fit and well.

We thought long and hard about this, and Peter changed his mind half a dozen times. In the end, he listened to the voice of the consultant and decided to go on holiday to France, which he loved, and have the operation ten days after our return.

The holiday was not a success. I had damaged my leg and could not go in the pool, which meant I could not sit in the sun because I need to leap into water after sunbathing. Peter was worried all the time about the operation and he said over and over again, 'I've stopped work and feel as fit as a fiddle. You and I are more loving than we have been for years, and I'm going to die.

After our return home, the operation day came, Peter's period in a Worthing clinic came to an end and he was allowed home six days later. On the day he came out, he ate well, felt fit and enjoyed himself. However, the next day he felt sick and did not want to eat or drink. In the early hours of the following morning, he woke me as he was being violently sick and suffering terrible pain.

I phoned the doctor, who came and gave him two huge painkillers—to a man who was being sick! I phoned him again half an hour later, he returned and called an ambulance to take Peter to Worthing General Hospital. To my shame, I didn't go with him because I was still in my night clothes and the ambulancemen were anxious to get him help as soon as possible.

I went to the hospital early the next morning and Peter was in the admissions ward, still obviously far from well. So I went home and returned in the evening. When I left, I kissed him goodbye and he said, 'Thank you for coming'—the last words he was to say to me.

At 10 pm, another consultant who had seen Peter before rang me to say that he was a very sick boy and they were going

to operate again. At midnight, he rang to let me know that the operation was over and Peter was in intensive care.

The next morning, I was at the hospital early and the anaesthetist in charge told me that Peter had septicaemia (diseased bacteria in the blood) and was very ill. I went to see him and there was my darling husband strung up with every instrument imaginable, unable to breathe for himself.

I rang Nigel, who was on an adventure holiday with Rosina and the children (by now, they had had a second son, Michael, three years David's junior), and he caught the next train. That night, Peter was very ill, but by the morning his blood pressure was rising and there was hope. Peter's brother came down from his home in the Lake District and we three unhappy people were at his bedside all day, every day.

The day came when the doctors announced that Peter's kidneys had failed and that he needed dialysis. They found him a bed in Portsmouth and we went over there, where they said they had to carry out another operation. Unbelievable. This was a fit man they were butchering. When we saw Peter after the operation, he was being kept alive by machines and the

246

doctors asked our permission to turn them off. We went and watched him die.

Peter had been my love of forty-two years. I'd loved him through thick and thin, good times and bad, and never looked at another man. Now he was gone and I had to go on alone. I didn't know how to face this. I did not cry—I was consumed by a terrible anger. How dare they do this to my wonderful man.

Nigel stayed as long as he could and was a great comfort and help to me. Brian did sterling work, too, phoning all our mutual friends and a lot of them came to Peter's cremation.

It was a lovely service. People came down from Leeds and Peter had what is called a good send-off. Brian gave an address, the emotion of it was too much. He broke down at the end. David, my grandson, read the following piece:

Children Learn What They Live

If a child lives with criticism
He learns to condemn

If a child lives with hostility
He learns to fight

If a child lives with ridicule
He learns to be shy

If a child lives with shame
He learns to feel guilty

If a child lives with tolerance
He learns to be patient

If a child lives with encouragement
He learns confidence

If a child lives with praise
He learns to appreciate

If a child lives with fairness
He learns justice

If a child lives with security
He learns to have faith

If a child lives with approval
He learns to like himself

If a child lives with acceptance and
friendship
He learns to find love in the world

My sister Nora stayed with me for two weeks, then had to go back home for her own health reasons. Rosina brought the children down for a day and we went on the beach. The sun shone and the children took off their shoes, followed by their socks, trousers, T-shirts and vests, then went for a paddle and a swim, enjoying a lovely day. It was a bonus day for me.

I did not know how to plan my future. Certainly, I decided, I would continue acting—Dr Theatre, as they say. Where would I live? I simply felt lost in a wilderness of indecision. I had to think about work. Everyone at Yorkshire Television was very good. They sent a car for me when needed and recorded all my scenes straight away, then I came home again.

Just as this terrible happening had torn my personal life apart, *Emmerdale* was about to celebrate its twenty-first anniversary, with my character at the centre of the storyline. I therefore had a busy schedule and made it clear that nothing should be changed.

My day for celebrating the programme's inception is 26 June because that was the date I started work on it, back in 1972.

But, of course, everyone else refers to 16 October, which was the date of the first transmission.

We had a wonderful party to celebrate the official anniversary, with Yorkshire Television taking over the whole of a very smart hotel. We had a marquee as well, with lots of champagne and good food. I did not know ninety per cent of the 400 people there. Goodness knows where they all came from!

Annie Sugden's life changed in the storyline, of course, with her decision to marry again following a proposal by wealthy Leonard Kempinski, a friend of Amos Brearly's who had wooed her while she was on one of her winter breaks in Spain.

Bernard Archard, who played Leonard, is a veteran character actor who starred in the long-running TV series *Spycatcher* in the fifties and sixties, and appeared in many films, including *Village of the Damned, The Day of the Jackal* and *The Sea Wolves.*

We had great fun preparing for the wedding and Bernard was a lovely person to act with. Kathy Tate (actress Malandra Burrows) helped Annie to pick her wedding

dress and a special hen night was arranged at The Woolpack for the bride, who even joked about the prospect of having a waterbed on her honeymoon!

When the big day arrived, I wore the hat that I had bought in real life for Nigel's wedding and had also worn at the 1983 Chelsea Flower Show—when I was presented with the Emmerdale Rose—and for Jean Rogers's wedding, as well as on TV for my screen son Joe's wedding. Yorkshire Television have bunged some awful hats on Annie's head from time to time, so I was determined to wear something that I knew suited me.

One lady wrote in to ask if it was the same hat that I wore at the Chelsea Flower Show. However, I didn't flatter myself that she remembered it from then—she had seen it in the previous issue of the *Emmerdale Magazine!*

Of course, the wedding did not go without a hitch or two. The guests arrived at the church in Beckindale to find the doors firmly locked. When new resident Vic Windsor finally managed to break open the door, another drama unfolded—Rev Johnson lost his voice. This was a perfect cue for Rev Donald Hinton, there as a

251

guest, to step in and take the service, to Annie's delight. This was also a happy occasion for me because it meant that Hugh Manning was making a brief return to the programme.

Filming the wedding was fun. The only trouble was that it started to rain cats and dogs, and the light went quickly, so we never finished the final scenes as written, with Annie throwing the flowers and son Jack's girlfriend Sarah catching them. Nor was there a close-up of the cake or the horseshoe in front of it, and no close-up of Annie.

So much for the wedding. Annie and Leonard moved into a house in Beckindale, then came disaster time. A new God arrived on the scene at *Emmerdale* in the form of Phil Redmond, the creator of *Grange Hill* and *Brookside*, who was taken on as the serial's consultant. Nicholas Prosser took over as producer, grabbed the programme by the scruff of the neck and rattled it so that several characters fell out.

As Christmas 1993 led into the New Year of 1994, we had to cope with a Lockerbie-style tragedy of a plane crashing over Beckindale and taking with it established cast members—Craig McKay

(who played my screen grandson, Mark Hughes), Tony Pitts (Archie Brooks) and Kate Dove (Elizabeth Feldmann)—as well as Bernard Archard, who acted Annie's short-lived second husband.

This event made all the cast very miserable, even though there was quite a thrill in doing something new and highly dramatic—at a cost of one million pounds to Yorkshire Television. Annie and Bernard were seen being driven by Joe to the airport for their winter break in Spain but, as the plane's debris shot all around, Joe swerved and the car crashed. Her new husband lay dead beside her. That was a terrible scene to do because I had so recently buried my own husband.

Annie, who was in a coma, had to go into intensive care for weeks on end, which again was quite traumatic after watching my husband die in intensive care. At least I knew the drill, with tubes and machines bleeping all over the place.

After three months, Annie came out of her coma as a result of Jack and Sarah bringing their new-born baby, Victoria, along to see her. That, of course, meant learning some lines again instead of just lying there or, some weeks, not being seen

on screen at all. This injection of new life in Beckindale, after the loss of lives in the air crash, was followed by Jack and Sarah's wedding and another chance for Annie to dress up.

With this event came the news too, that the village of Beckindale was to be renamed Emmerdale following the disaster, largely because Emmerdale Farm had been the centre of the community for so long and Annie Sugden was held in such high esteem.

12
Supporting Players

A few years ago, I cut down my work on *Emmerdale* to one week in every month. Because the programme records its studio scenes one week and the location shots the following week, it meant I could actually be seen on screen two weeks in every four. Working on location is too much for me now, in my seventies, and I was also given three months off during the winter because I was not up to travelling more than 300 miles to the studios from my home any more. However, the dramas of the plane crash demanded that I went up more often during that winter of great change in the programme.

I had remained busy during the weeks when I was not working on *Emmerdale*, keeping the house as clean as I could with Peter around—he was very untidy! I would also visit friends and go to WeightWatchers and swimming aquatic therapy, for people who have something wrong with their

bones. As I've got older, I cannot walk down the stairs so easily and getting up from a sitting-down position hurts my knees.

But I should be thankful for my health as it is, for my elder brother Malcolm died a couple of years ago at the age of eighty and Brian has had a new heart valve. Brian, of course, followed a successful career as an actor-manager by becoming involved in MENCAP, the charity for the mentally handicapped, eventually being appointed its secretary-general.

That surprising event came about as a result of Brian and Elspet's first daughter, Shelley, being born a Down's syndrome baby. Little was known then about mongolism, as it was called back in 1951, and they were persuaded that it was best to have Shelley brought up in a home for the mentally handicapped. That meant going through the awful process of having her certified, something that changed shortly afterwards, thankfully, largely as a result of parental pressure. But such was the ignorance then about the condition that Brian was even asked whether he had VD or was drunk at the time of conception.

From the age of five, Shelley lived just a short distance away, so Brian and Elspet were able to see her regularly. As Brian's interest and support for various relevant charities increased over the years, so did research into the subject, and MENCAP grew into the champion of those suffering from various mental handicaps.

Brian had, in fact, followed his stage career in 1977 by becoming theatre controller for Ray Cooney and Laurie Marsh, placing productions in venues owned by Cooney-Marsh Theatres and being responsible for their overall management. The move was not entirely successful. Brian did not enjoy the work and was left wondering what to do with the rest of his life when he saw an advertisement for the job of MENCAP secretary-general, which he succeeded in getting. During seven years in that capacity, he backed improvements in care of the handicapped and used his high media profile to raise awareness of the subject of mental handicap.

Although he retired from MENCAP in 1987, Brian became its chairman the following year. He also returned to the stage by starring in a revival of *Dry Rot* at

the Lyric Theatre in London's West End, this time playing not his original role of bookie's runner Fred Phipps, but that of the bookie, Alf Tubbe. It proved to be a massive success and he decided to finish his acting career on a high note.

Brian is now retired and, in addition to his CBE and knighthood, was made Lord Rix of Whitehall in the City and Hornsea in 1992. His second daughter, Louisa, is a successful actress herself, starring on television in *Colin's Sandwich*, opposite Mel Smith, and the comedy series *Side by Side*, and his son Jamie works in television production—in fact, he was associate producer of *Colin's Sandwich*. Brian and Elspet's second son, Jonathan, is a writer, so the family is carrying on the Rix theatrical tradition that Brian and I started.

My son, Nigel, has followed nine years working in the BBC's video engineering department by joining LWT as a sound engineer and video editor, and is very content there. He was so good-looking, though, and such a good mimic that he probably could have made it in acting. However, we never encouraged him because an actor's life is a precarious

one and we knew the heartache of going to work only nights and leaving the little chap with babysitters or mother's helps, some good, some downright bad.

Nigel had never shown any inclination to go into the theatre and was always interested in electronics. He went to university but hated the academic life. A rail strike came and he couldn't get to college, so decided not to go any more, wrote to the BBC and landed a job completely off his own bat.

He's a practical person, a great DIY buff—all he does not do is bricks and mortar. At all three houses in which he and Rosina have lived, he has done some fantastic work, even plumbing in his own bathroom because he believes he can do it better than any plumber! He is something of a perfectionist.

Now, Nigel and Rosina live in the Kent countryside and keep chickens, ducks, guinea pigs and sheep. Rosina spends her life rushing around looking after all the animals and children—fetching the boys from school and doing a thousand and one jobs for other people. She is the strongest woman I have ever known and has so much energy that she never seems to sit down.

259

One person with whom I was reunited after several decades was Charles, the Desert Rat to whom I was engaged during the war. I wrote to him back in the sixties because it was the twenty-fifth anniversary of our engagement—Bastille Day, in fact—and we had not kept in touch since I failed to respond to his wartime message that he had set a date for our wedding. I simply told him that it was time I heard from him and gave him all my family news.

Sure enough, he replied. 'I think after twenty-five years we can open the box of memories,' he wrote. So we started to correspond and sometimes he would phone me and say, 'I was looking out of my window in the office, with the blue sky and lovely sunshine, and it made me think of joy and of you.'

We had some lovely conversations. However, he retired from his job and obviously could not phone from home because he had a wife, so those happy conversations ceased. A long time later, he telephoned our house in Shepperton and spoke to Peter, saying that he was in Britain and would love to see me. Peter told him to come up to Leeds and stay because

we had plenty of spare beds there.

He came up to see me and we drank champagne, went out to dinner, came home, drank brandy and talked into the early hours. Then, he said in his wonderful French accent, 'Would you like to sleep in my arms tonight, darling?' I had been expecting this, but it was still a shock. I told him I would love to, but I had been faithful to my husband for more than thirty years and did not want to break that faith.

Charles was very nice, but the next morning he clearly expected me to leap into bed with him, which I didn't, and he left an hour later angry. What a long way for nothing! And I have not heard from him since. It is so sad because ours had been such a lovely relationship.

Which leaves Janet, the child I had and was forced to give away for adoption. Sadly, her husband Oliver died of cancer following a brave fight, just seven months after my beloved Peter died, so we are both widows.

The sad thing was that, through his hypnotherapy career, Peter had accepted the fact that Janet existed and we had arranged to go to see them in Devon.

Alas, Oliver was too ill and the visit was postponed again. Alas, once more, Peter died before we had set another date and I did not see Oliver again.

Brian and Elspet went to the funeral in Devon. Both of them were very fond of Janet and wished I had seen more of her of late. Now, Janet is to come and stay with me and meet again her half-brother, Nigel, and his children, so the circle will be complete.

Now, I must concentrate on my own grand-children, both of whom are naughty darlings. I adore them and they both did so well recently in their recitations at the Hastings Festival. David won a mask as the child who had shown promise, work and attitude, and Michael came fourth out of thirty entrants in the category of beautiful articulation and quality, in spite of having a slight speech impediment.

I see both of my grandchildren as often as I can and they sometimes come to my house for a day's swimming in the pool. Provided the water is warm, they will go in the pool in any weather and are both expert swimmers for their age. My life is now much clearer. I know I must go on working as long as I can, if only to bring

a few luxuries to those two ragamuffins.

I'm still enjoying my work on *Emmerdale*, although I preferred playing Annie in the old days, when I had a lot of dramatic scenes. In the early years, many of those were with Toke Townley, playing my screen father. His death meant that they were virtually halved and, more recently, Arthur Pentelow's sudden death has given me less to do, although Annie's wedding and subsequent coma did put her right back in the spotlight.

In the beginning, *Emmerdale* was watched mostly by mothers with babies, as well as anyone who went home for their lunch. Now, it's on at peak time and has a much wider audience. However, the programme has maintained high standards over more than twenty years. It seems to be a mixture of the characterisations and the humour—there's always something funny going on. That's the same with *Coronation Street*, which is superb comedy and drama, and a programme I never miss.

I have been with the character of Annie for more than twenty years. After her second, short-lived marriage, I asked for Annie to have her name changed back to Sugden. Annie Kempinski never really felt

right. It was a nice little story while it lasted, but the marriage was all too brief for anyone to remember.

Living and working in Yorkshire for much of the time, I tend almost to think in Yorkshire, just as when in France I try to think in French. But, by the time I've been back in my Sussex home for a couple of weeks, that's gone.

As for ambitions, I don't really have any left. Many of the parts I wanted to play I did while acting in rep and, although some people would say that it was only rep and not appearing in front of millions on television, the most important thing was to get it out of my system then. I would like to have done more Shakespeare, though, and I still read a lot of his works.

I sold my house in Leeds because I was so lonely on my own, with Peter always down South and no longer having my dog, Cassius, for company. Now, of course, Peter has gone. I would love to continue working on *Emmerdale* until I drop. I'm so happy when I'm actually working. What I love is the companionship and the fun we have. I've been a working woman for so long I don't really know what it's like to sit back and do nothing.

Appendices

THEATRE
Rep at the Grand Theatre, Hull (1939):
Death Takes a Holiday
Little Ladyship
Murder Has Been Arranged
Without the Prince

Donald Wolfit Shakespeare Company tour (autumn 1939):
Hamlet
Othello
The Merchant of Venice
Twelfth Night
The Taming of the Shrew
Julius Caesar

Reunion Theatre tour of Germany (1946):
Exercise Bowler (Mrs Moss)

National tour (1947):
Old Mother Riley and Her Daughter Kitty
  (Mrs Ginnocci)

Repertory theatre (1947–52)

The following is not comprehensive. Working in repertory theatre during its heyday inevitably meant that I appeared in hundreds of productions, too many to list here, and played many roles long forgotten.

Theatre Royal, Warrington (1947):
The Man Who Came to Dinner
Smiling Through
East Lynne
This is My Life
The Poltergeist

De La Warr Pavilion, Bexhill (1948):
Thunder Rock
Sarah Simple

Repertory Theatre, Tonbridge (1948):
Frieda

King's Hall, Ilkley (1948):
The Eagle Has Two Heads
Portrait in Black

The Hippodrome, Margate (1949):
Jupiter Laughs (Fanny Deeming, the Matron)
French for Love

266

Spa Theatre, Bridlington (1949):
Summer in December (Elspeth French)
The Corn is Green (Miss Moffat)

Grand Pavilion, Bridlington (1949–50):
Playbill: A Harlequinade (Edna Selby)
The Giaconda Smile (Janet Spence)
The Chiltern Hundreds (The Countess of Lister)
Murder Me Please (Emily Holt)
Don't Listen, Ladies! (Valentine)
The Blind Goddess
When We Are Married (Maria Helliwell)
September Tide (Stella Martyn)
Saloon Bar (Doris)
East Lynne (Lady Isabel)
We Proudly Present (Sandra Mars)
Lovers' Lane (Helen Storer)
Babes in the Wood (The Good Fairy)
The Girl Who Couldn't Quite (Pam Taylor)
The Happiest Days of Your Life (Miss Evelyn Whitchurch)
The Perfect Woman (Lady Geviphie)
Hong Kong Cocktail (Lady Suzette Tyepanne)
By Adoption (Drusilla)
This Happy Breed (Sylvia)

Spa Theatre, Bridlington (1950):
Ma's Bit 0' Brass (Mrs Lovejoy)
Present Laughter (Liz Essendine)
Yes and No (Emma Jarrow)
The Rotters (Mrs Clugston)

Theatre Royal, Huddersfield (1951):
Castle in the Air ('Boss' Trent)
September Tide (Stella Martyn)
Magic Slippers (Agatha Granger)
George & Margaret (Beer)
Victoria Regina (The Duchess of Kent, A Duchess and Her Royal Highness the Princess of Wales)
One Wild Oat (Lydia Gilbey)
Candida (Candida)
Harvey (Mrs Ethel Chaurenet)
The Sacred Flame (Nurse Wayland)
The Perfect Woman (Lady Geviphie)
The Winslow Boy (Catherine Winslow)
Autumn Crocus (The Lady in Spectacles)
Rookery Nook (Gertrude Twine)
Edward My Son (Evelyn Holt)

Theatre Royal, Huddersfield (1952):
On Monday Next (Sandra Layton)
Charley's Uncle (Bubbles Merton)
Sweet Aloes

The Letter
Pygmalion (Mrs Higgins)

London West End farces (1956–69)
Dry Rot, Whitehall Theatre, 1956–8 (The Colonel's Lady)
Simple Spymen, Whitehall Theatre, 1958–61 (Mrs Byng)
One for the Pot, Whitehall Theatre, 1961–4 (Aunt Amy)
Chase Me, Comrade!, Whitehall Theatre, 1964–6 (Mrs Riddington), plus 1966 summer season in Morecambe and national tour
Stand By Your Bedouin (Louise)/*Uproar in the House* (House Guest), Garrick Theatre, 1967
Uproar in the House, Whitehall Theatre, 1967–9 (House Guest)

'Six of Rix' national tour (1972)
A Spot of Bother
Aren't Men Beasts!
Madame Louise
One Wild Oat
Will Any Gentleman?
What the Dr Ordered

FILMS

The Night We Dropped a Clanger, Rank, 1959

The Night We Got the Bird, British Lion, 1960

TELEVISION

Exercise Bowler, BBC, 1946 (Mrs Moss)
  Various one-off farces with the Whitehall Theatre company, BBC

Dial Rix (nine episodes), BBC, 1962

Six of Rix (six episodes), BBC 1, 1972

Emmerdale Farm, ITV, 1972– *(Emmerdale* since 1989) (Annie Sugden)

Whose Baby?, ITV, 1983

This is Your Life (subject), ITV, 1985

ITV Telethon '92, ITV, 1992

Good Morning Britain, ITV, 1992

The publishers hope that this book has given you enjoyable reading. Large Print Books are especially designed to be as easy to see and hold as possible. If you wish a complete list of our books, please ask at your local library or write directly to: Magna Large Print Books, Long Preston, North Yorkshire, BD23 4ND, England.

This Large Print Book for the Partially sighted, who cannot read normal print, is published under the auspices of

THE ULVERSCROFT FOUNDATION

THE ULVERSCROFT FOUNDATION

. . . we hope that you have enjoyed this Large Print Book. Please think for a moment about those people who have worse eyesight problems than you . . . and are unable to even read or enjoy Large Print, without great difficulty.

You can help them by sending a donation, large or small to:

**The Ulverscroft Foundation,
1, The Green, Bradgate Road,
Anstey, Leicestershire, LE7 7FU,
England.**
or request a copy of our brochure for more details.

The Foundation will use all your help to assist those people who are handicapped . by various sight problems and need special attention.

Thank you very much for your help.

ANNIE'S SONG
My Life & Emmerdale

You know her as Annie Sugden, the indomitable matriarch of Emmerdale, a role which she has played for over twenty years. But actress Sheila Mercier has played many roles in her eventful life, some more heartbreaking than anything seen on the screen. Here she tells her own story about her wealthy background; her broken engagement to a French Desert Rat; how she helped her brother Brian Rix achieve theatrical success, and her experiences on Emmerdale and the people and stories on the screen and behind-the-scenes.

ANNIE'S SONG
My Life & Emmerdale

by
Sheila Mercier
with Anthony Hayward

Magna Large Print Books
Long Preston, North Yorkshire,
England.

British Library Cataloguing in Publication Data.

Mercier, Sheila and Hayward, Anthony
    Annie's song: my life & Emmerdale.

    A catalogue record for this book is
    available from the British Library

    ISBN 0-7505-0847-7

First published in Great Britain by Titan Books, 1994

Published in Large Print October, 1995 by arrangement with Titan Books Ltd.

Magna Large Print is an imprint of
Library Magna Books Ltd.
Printed and bound in Great Britain by
T.J. Press (Padstow) Ltd., Cornwall, PL28 8RW.

CONTENTS

CONTENTS

**For Peter, my beloved husband
of forty-two years**

Foreword
by Brian Rix
Lord Rix of Whitehall, CBE, DL

There is an old theatrical expedient—nepotism—that stood many an actor in good stead in days of yore. In the 1840s, the Lincoln Circuit was run by a Mr and Mrs Robertson, who had seventeen children to call upon, including Dame Madge Kendal, while in other parts of the country the Terry family had eleven acting offspring, including Dame Ellen, and the Kembles had a useful twelve, including Sarah Siddons, who was too early to be created a Dame of the British Empire—she was still a rogue and a vagabond. Then there are the Wyndhams, the Alberys, the Barrymores, the Redgraves, the Comptons, the Forbes-Robertsons, the Jerrolds, the Lupinos, the Maudes, the Rathbones, the Thorndikes, and so on and so on...

The Rixes are very small beer compared with those great hereditary theatrical families, for our numbers are limited and we

11

cover only two generations anyway. My sister, Sheila, was the first to become a professional actor—and her decision led to my decline and fall a few years later. Mind you, there was a war on, I was waiting to go into the RAF, Sheila had introduced me to her first boss, Donald Wolfit, and, because young actors were in short supply in those wartime days, the rest was easy: Wolfit became my boss too.

It was our mother's fault really. She was mad on the theatre, had a very sweet soprano voice, which she used to good effect in the local amateur operatic society, started a concert party (Mrs Fanny Rix And Her Bright Young Things) to support the church and local charities, went on to produce Passion Plays at Easter and then five or six plays a year, which were very successful in the Parish Hall or the Floral Hall or Granville Court, Hornsea. Not the grandest of venues, but at least it was a start, and all her children—Malcolm, Nora, Sheila and I—were dragged in to take part. Being the youngest, I was generally a stage manager—but Sheila and co basked in local stardom. My turn came later.

Sheila then went to drama college in Stratford-upon-Avon, under the tutelage

12

of the finest King Lear of his day, Randle Ayrton, and was contracted by Donald Wolfit, and so the story begins. After the Second World War was over, I was demobbed as an out-of-work actor, borrowed some money from my father and uncle, started my own company and was on my way as an actor-manager—a role I was to occupy for the next thirty years. Naturally, I wanted my sister with me (it's always safer to have your own family around if you can't pay the wages!) and, although Sheila was not keen, she eventually joined me in Ilkley. This was followed by Bridlington, Margate and, finally, the Whitehall Theatre, after she had met and married Peter Mercier, when the two of them joined me in London. It was then that Sheila adopted her married name, Mercier, for we both felt that one Rix was enough in the programme, especially because my brother-in-law (Peter) was working with me, as well as my wife, Elspet (Gray), while Elspet's sister, Rhoda, designed all my sets, for both theatre and television. Years later, I was to act with our daughter, Louisa (who has kept Rix as her stage name), while our sons, Jamie and Jonathan, went

into the profession somewhat tangentially, for both are writers, although Jamie is also a producer and director in the world of television. As for Sheila's son, Nigel, he, too, went into telly—but as a technician, not an artist.

No need to tell you any more, really—it's all in the book. Oh, except one little thing—Sheila has always been a jolly good sister to me and I hope this autobiography sells well, apart from showing what a kind person she is and how she deserves her success. The only snag is her name. Once, Sheila Rix; then, Sheila Mercier; now, for millions of viewers, plain Annie Sugden. Maybe all three should be credited with writing this book—quite apart from Anthony Hayward!

Brian Rix

14

Preface

It was Millie, my dresser at Yorkshire Television, who said, 'Why don't you write a book?' During more than twenty years of working on *Emmerdale*, she had heard me talking about all sorts of things that had happened during a lifetime in showbusiness. Millie has been my dresser for so long now that I look on her as my best friend. She is always there when needed and puts up with my bad temper when changing clothes and when I can't get something off or on—and always with a smile. When she is away, I feel positively deprived.

One day, I returned to my dressing-room to find her with some paper and a ball-point pen with a feather attached to it so that it looked like a quill pen. She handed it to me and said, 'Write.'

What follows are the results, and during the time I have spent working on this book many happy memories and recollections of old friends have come flooding back to me.

15

There have been some sad memories, too, but they all go to make up a life that has certainly been full.

I would like to thank Shanti Bhatia, who helped to make this book possible by putting me in contact with Anthony Hayward, who collaborated with me on the writing.

Sheila Mercier

16

I
Early Stages

The sea has been near for much of my life. I was brought up next to it in the East Riding of Yorkshire and now live on the Sussex coast. It was the source of my family's wealth, for at the age of eleven my grandfather ran away from home and built a ship, the *UR&M*, with his own hands in the harbour at Burnham Overy Staithe in Norfolk. From that sprang the firm of Robert Rix & Sons, shipowners and brokers, with offices in Hull, an industrial city that sits on the River Humber as it widens and makes its way out to the cruel North Sea.

My grandfather was a lion of a man, with an imposing, fifty-four-inch chest. His ships carried J. Arthur Rank's flour and the two helped each other on the ladder to success. Rank, the flour magnate, was also father of the man who was to become king of the British motion-picture industry, as a producer, distributor and cinema owner,

17

with some of the country's most famous films bearing his name and the famous gong symbol.

The Rix family had lived in Norfolk for hundreds of years, moving from Hindolveston to Wells-next-the Sea. Robert left Wells for Stockton in about 1860 and his family moved north to Hull several decades later. My father, Herbert Dobson Rix—one of eight children and always referred to as 'HD'—joined the family shipping firm, along with elder brothers John Robert ('JR') and Ernest Bertram ('EB'). At one time, they owned fourteen ships, all of them engaged in trade around the English coast or relatively close places on the Continent. All the fleet of ships had names ending in 'Rix', so there was RobRix, KenRix, LesRix, MalRix (an unlucky ship) and NorRix. They stopped before they got to SheRix and BriRix (me and my brother Brian)! The company still exists today, run by a cousin, and since moving to Sussex I have spotted the SalRix carrying stones from Cornwall to Littlehampton along the coast.

My grandfather on the other side of the family was the youngest of sixteen children, of whom fourteen died before reaching the

age of twenty-one, including all the girls, who died in childbirth. My mother, Fanny Nicholson, had seven brothers and sisters, all of them brought up strictly. Her father would sit at the dinner table with a cane and rap over the knuckles anyone who was naughty, which was enough to keep them in order.

His wife, my grandmother, was of Welsh descent, born a Roberts. I do not think she came from Wales herself because she did not have the accent, but the Welsh blood has certainly been passed on as Brian and I had the dark colouring you would associate with the race. Anyway, I've no idea how my mother and father met, but they married and bore a son, Malcolm, and a daughter, Nora. Then, I was born, Sheila Betty Rix, at our home on Beverley High Road, in Hull, on I January 1919, into a world that has now disappeared.

Being well-off, we had two maids, a nanny, a gardener, a governess and a washer-woman. When we wanted a piece of coal put on the fire, we rang a bell for a maid to come and carry out the arduous task. Our parents figured little in our early lives, for we children lived upstairs in the nursery, looked after by our nanny. The

only exceptions were Sundays, when the whole family would sit down to lunch, or when we were naughty and had to be thrashed—and Mummy had a wicked hand for walloping. I certainly had a few smacks in my time! For Sunday lunch, we had Yorkshire pudding with onion gravy as a starter and whoever ate the most had more meat for their main course. My mother always carved. I don't know why, but she did.

When I was two, we moved to nearby Cottingham. Whereas Hull was a big, throbbing city, Cottingham was in the heart of the countryside. You had to walk twenty minutes to get a tram to go into Hull. Our new house was the making of childhood dreams, large and semi-detached, with a big garden, tennis courts and summer-houses—a wonderful place to grow up because there was so much space and so many nooks and crannies, ideal for endless games of hide-and-seek.

Between us and the house next door was a very high wall, which we used to practise our tennis strokes. There was also laid-on entertainment, because our next-door neighbours owned a monkey that used to run along the top of the wall and scream

insults at us in the yard below.

The garden was lovely and our full-time gardener, old John, produced every vegetable and fruit imaginable. We even had our own chickens, so we were very self-sufficient.

My first vivid memory is of my sister, Nora, and I being bridesmaids at cousin Walter's wedding. We were dressed as primroses and, as the service progressed, I turned to the grown-up bridesmaid behind me and told her I wanted to go to the loo. She said I couldn't, so I responded with noisy tears and a puddle in the centre of the aisle, which the bride promptly stepped in on her way out. I also ruined all the photographs afterwards, yelling with my mouth wide open. Perhaps not the best of first memories to have!

Before going to school, we had a governess, whom we all hated. She tried to teach me fractions at the tender age of three-and-a-half. No wonder I'm no good at maths! Eventually, we were sent to Miss Milner's kindergarten, where there was an awful boy called Bertil Gumbolt, who teased me dreadfully.

Many years later, when fame as Annie Sugden led me to signing *Emmerdale* books

in Hull, a man came up to me and asked whether I could remember anyone from that kindergarten. 'Yes,' I replied, 'I remember Bertil Gumbolt. He put an earwig down my back.' To which this man replied, '*I* am Bertil Gumbolt.' He used to wear velvet suits with beads on them at school. I don't know why we didn't tease him about that!

When Mummy fell pregnant, we were told to pray for a little brother, and found our prayers had been answered when, one morning, Daddy came into the nursery in his dressing gown—a rare event—and announced Brian's birth.

We were allowed to see the little fellow in his cot in our parents' bedroom and couldn't understand why Mummy was in bed. She wasn't ill and, after all, the doctor had brought Brian in his little black bag after taking one look at the baby, who had fallen from Heaven, and deciding it resembled our mother.

I was only five at the time, and my sister was two years older, but we knew exactly how to bring up babies, for we played endlessly with our dolls, dressing them, undressing them, bathing them, putting them to bed and pushing their prams for

long walks in the countryside.

Brian says his first memory of me was sitting on one end of the see-saw in the garden when he was three or four. Nora was on the other end and Brian was unlucky enough to have his finger squashed under the see-saw. Another time, he recalls, one of us trapped his finger in a door. Poor Brian! He seemed beset with injury and illness during his childhood, worst of all when he went down with measles at the age of eight. In those days, measles could be fatal and it still affects Brian as he contracted sinusitis. At the time, it was touch and go whether he would develop mastoiditis, because his ears were badly affected by the measles. Today, he's kind enough to credit me as the attentive sister, nursing him back to health, putting hot wads of cotton wool on his ears.

Brian had a nanny called Miss Allin, whom I christened Allie one day. The name stuck and she remained Allie until the day she died. She went with us on family holidays to Filey, which was a wonderful place for children in those days, with so much going on. There were the Pierrots, who seemed to perform whatever

the weather, the Salvation Army, with whom we sang hymns, Punch and Judy shows and donkey rides. I always, rather grandly, had a chariot on the beach.

Then there was the magic of Filey brigg, which apparently goes out for miles under the sea. At low tide, it was full of sea flowers, crabs and shellfish, which we would collect, before running away as the waves pounded against the brigg—whoever got wet was a cissy! Brian was a baby when we went to Filey, where the town was high up above the beach. The only drawback was pushing his pram back to our hotel at the end of the day.

Back home at about that time, Brian had a bad attack of whooping cough. I nursed him and, every time he was sick, I banged on the nursery floor for Allie to come and clear up the mess. Fortunately, he survived it, as he did the episode of swallowing paint stored in a garden shed. I will never forget the panic on Allie's face as she sat forcing mustard down his throat to make him sick. Of course, paint then contained lead and was highly toxic.

The nursery was the scene of other notable events, too. In those days, if you had an operation, it was fashionable for

the surgeon to come to you. At the age of seven, I had my tonsils and adenoids removed on the nursery table, and Dr Ridgy Rogers was the unfortunate surgeon who had the task of performing this minor operation. It turned into a struggle, with my knee clocking him on the chin. Afterwards, Allie sat and stroked my forehead, Mummy made some delicious ice-cream and my favourite cousin, Kenneth, brought me a painting book. It was all worth the pain to get this sort of attention!

Later, I woke up one day feeling very strange and screaming, 'I'm going to die, I'm going to die!' Allie took me into the nursery and rocked me on her knee until I had calmed down. When Nora and I went to a French convent school in Hull, those peculiar feelings returned. I would cry, gasp for breath and feel weak. Once, the Reverend Mother took me into the kitchen, put me on the table and gave me an almighty whack. The doctor came and could find nothing wrong, so I was taught a prayer that I had to say whenever the feelings came on: 'Please, Jesus, make me a good little girl and don't let me think all those silly things.' Time passed and I gradually grew out of it. I suppose today

they would be called panic attacks.

I was a very shy child, terrified of everything. We wore extremely frilly knickers in those days and I would worry that they were showing. I hated walks by the pond, scared that I might fall in, even though it was quite a way from the road, and I was also wary of aeroplanes flying overhead. Nora and I were both very gullible and believed everything we were told. Something that struck terror in our hearts was the 'news' that all the big houses behind walls in our road were occupied by ogresses, and we used to run past them, filled with fear.

When I was ten, my parents moved from Cottingham to Hornsea, just two minutes' walk from the sea. It was then that Nora and I no longer had nannies and lived and dined with our parents, getting to know them for the first time. Daddy was a very gentle man. When we cried at night, it was always he who got out of bed, came to us and patted the eiderdown round us to make us comfortable. However, like all gentle people, he had a violent side. He and Mummy used to have great rows, especially at breakfast, and many is the time the marmalade pot went whizzing at

Mummy. She always dodged it and the marmalade would land on the dining-room wall. Then, Daddy would walk out through the back door and Mummy would leave through the front one, only to return half-an-hour later as if nothing had happened.

But Daddy adored Mummy and thought she was beautiful—which she was—and said there was no one like her. He was handsome but shy, whereas Mummy was outgoing and could be very nasty towards him. She hated him smoking a pipe and leaving his tobacco and matches everywhere.

Hillcrest, our house at Hornsea, was a lovely place to live, with a tennis court to play on and one of the attics turned into a gym. So we were quite healthy and went to the beach as often as possible, dashing in and out of the rough sea whatever the weather—hail, rain, snow or high wind. Poor Allie, Brian's nanny, used to sit up against the sea wall wrapped in rugs and mackintoshes. She must have wished us miles away.

We already knew Hornsea quite well because Miss Harker—my nanny until the age of four-and-a-half—lived there and we would often stay at her mother's

boarding-house. Once, I was bitten by their seventeen-year-old West Highland terrier. Running into the kitchen, I bumped into Nanny Harker's mother, who was carrying a plate of fish, which resulted in the dish breaking and me cutting my forehead. I was held down as they poured iodine into the wound and I still have the scar. We loved Nanny Harker and continued to visit her every week until the day she died.

Our days at the convent school had been lovely. We played tennis and croquet, and Reverend Mother's Feast Day was particularly memorable. It was a holiday event, with stalls offering tantalising things to buy—my favourites were French bonbons. Making daisy chains was a fine summer-time way of passing the hours and we would lie on the lawn on hot days, garlanded with them.

But it was too far to commute daily to school from Hornsea, so we were sent to the convent as weekly boarders for two terms. We had to provide our own cutlery and silver mugs, cakes and biscuits, jam and marmalade.

We were so unhappy boarding, and the food was so awful, that we left and went to St Ethelburga's in Hornsea, sister

prep school of St Bede's, where Brian went. His headmaster was 'Bickie'—Dr G. H. Bickmore, who kept in touch with my brother all his life and appeared on television the first time Brian was the subject of *This is Your Life*.

They were wonderful teachers at St Ethelburga's, and Nora and I were thoroughly happy. I recently dug out my school report from Michaelmas term, 1930, when I was almost twelve: 'Sheila is doing well, especially in languages. She has a very quick mind and applies herself to her work.' And, sure enough, it showed that I had come first in both French and Latin. It was at St Ethelburga's that I had my first elocution lessons, and it was my elocution teacher, Miss Doris Watt, who told me that I should go on the stage.

My first chance of glory came when the school put on a production of *The Windmill Man*, with a cast featuring a multitude of both grown-ups and children. It is a magical play that I had first seen in Hull and, regrettably, is rarely performed these days. I still have the score and the libretto, and have tried to persuade both the BBC and Yorkshire Television to record it, but they said it would be too expensive

to produce. Expensive! When our little school did it, all the teachers and almost all the girls took part. It was a fantastic production. I played the leading boy, the Prince, and Nora was the Princess.

Among my lines was one that I could never bring myself to utter: 'I do believe at last I'm going to cry.' I said all the boys would think I was a cissy. So, on the first night, I was bribed with a box of chocolates to say the line, which I did for that night only. For the rest of the week, I just mumbled it. It was a really happy time and I still remember all the songs and the music after all these years.

Then, my parents moved again, just down the road in Hornsea to a house called Kirkdale. It had three reception rooms, one of them with a parquet floor where we used to roll back the carpet and dance. The house was always full of young people enjoying themselves. How our parents put up with the noise I shall never know.

My elder brother, Malcolm, used to play rugby for Hornsea and would bring opponents home for a bath. One Saturday, he brought back three Cameron High-landers. I swooned at the sight of these

gorgeous hunks, but my dear father said, 'Oh, Sheila isn't interested in men—she only cares about the theatre.' I could have crowned him! Alas, the time came for us to start growing up, and Nora and I were sent to Hunmanby Hall, high up on the Yorkshire Moors. Malcolm had attended Wrekin College, in Shropshire, but had frequently been ill, which resulted in my parents dashing across the country to see him, so they vowed that we would go to a boarding-school nearer home. It was the fashion for children to be sent away to boarding-school in those days, especially among the well-off.

Hunmanby Hall, although a cold, cold place on the moors, was very beautiful, boasting an amazing history, spacious grounds and comfortable, new buildings. Each dormitory, housing about twenty girls, had a cubicle for each and a teacher in a room at the end.

What a contrast to St Ethelburga's, though. How I hated my schooldays now. I was terrified of doing something wrong, getting a disorder mark and having my name read out in front of everyone at breakfast the following morning. It was a misplaced fear, because I had only two

31

disorder marks during my whole time there. I used to write home, 'Mummy, how I long for the days when I sat with you in front of the fire.' Of course, it had never been like that! At school, we played sports every day. In the winter, it was hockey, and I can still feel the pain of the cold wind in my ears. Summer I enjoyed because we played tennis, which I loved, and cricket, which all Yorkshire folk follow with pride.

My elocution lessons continued, and when school plays came round I was always in them. I certainly didn't shine academically. In fact, my geometry paper for a maths exam for matric went back empty. I did like French and, believe it or not, Latin. Years later, when my son was learning Latin, I used to help him with his homework and learned it all over again!

While at school, I was very ignorant about sex and nobody else seemed to be any wiser. I missed 'the curse' once when I was fourteen and wrote home to tell Mummy. I thought I must be having a baby. This resulted in her rushing to the school with her doctor friends, walking me down the drive and telling me that if ever a man tried to do anything to me to kick

him 'there'—but she never told me where 'there' was, so again I was none the wiser. There was no baby, of course, and a bottle of iron tonic put the problem right.

At the age of fourteen, I fell in love while on a family holiday to Weybridge, in Surrey, which from Yorkshire was a long way to travel then and few people would go that far. The boy's name was Brian and he was the son of a famous writer called Ian Walmsley, who lived in Robin Hood's Bay on the Yorkshire coast—apparently named so not because of any link with the famous English folk hero, whose activities are reputed to have been centred further south in Nottinghamshire, but because of the smuggling that once went on there.

Brian was certainly a handsome man, but really too grown-up for me. I was fourteen and he was nineteen. We never even kissed because we were brought up to think that kissing was something that nice girls didn't do. I wrote to him once or twice afterwards but soon forgot him when I was back at school, although the memory lingers on.

Carl Brisson, a famous Danish film star of the time who acted in Britain, was also staying at the hotel in Weybridge with

his very elegant lady and a fox—which was rather eccentric and something that would certainly not be allowed in hotels today. One day, the naughty fox ran away and all the children were sent into the woods to find it! What we would have done if confronted with the fox, Lord only knows!

That was a boiling-hot fortnight and we spent most of the time round the hotel pool. I shared a room with Nora near a belfry and had all the windows open at night because of the heat. When we spotted six bats in our bedroom, we ran down to get Daddy, who came up with a tennis racquet and bowler hat—to keep the bats out of his hair—and proceeded to evict them with his skilled backhand. We spent the rest of the two weeks with the windows closed—boiling.

Our holidays were always in England and spent in hotels, from where we could walk miles, visit castles and churches, and even go blackberry-picking, so that we could take the fruit back and make tarts.

Back home in Hornsea, we would have a bathing tent on the beach every summer. It all sounds so old and Victorian now, but that's what people did then, and the

summers were so long and so hot. That's the way it seemed, anyway, throughout the thirties, when many other people around the country were facing such gloomy times and finding few prospects for themselves in the job market.

On leaving school at the age of sixteen, I had to decide what I wanted to do and opted for a year off to enjoy myself. I found work in a stables, where I learnt to ride. Hornsea was a lovely place to be on horseback because you could go on the beach and jump the breakwaters, which were often a bit hairy, high on one side and low on the other. Fortunately, the horses loved splashing through the waves. I used to muck-out, clean brasses and polish leather, and loved every minute of it.

My riding mistress, Betty Ramsden, wanted a dog to follow the horses, so she bought a blue roan cocker spaniel called Flush. Our family had owned a string of dogs, from Jock the Aberdeen terrier to child-loving Peter, our first Airedale, who came to an untimely end when he fought the dogs on a nearby farm and was shot by the farmer. There were also our rough-haired terriers, all called Tim. The second one adored ice-cream and would sit next to

Mr Phillips's stall on the front at Hornsea every day throughout the summer, begging until he was given a halfpenny cornet.

At the stables, I soon made friends with Flush. On his first night there, I rode by on my bike and heard him crying. So I climbed the wall and rescued the dog, putting him to sleep in my doll's cot, which I retrieved from the loft. From that day, he loved only me, and Betty eventually said, 'Take him—he's your dog.' Never was a dog so adored and he did everything he was told. His favourite trick was to sing. 'Sing, Flush,' we used to say, and he would lift his head and sing until we stopped him. I still remember a holiday we took in Cromer on the Norfolk coast. The hotel we were staying at had a goldfish pond and Flush would sit for hours with his enormous ears dangling into the water, hoping to do the impossible and catch one. It was also there that I found a boyfriend called Felix, who came from Potters Bar, in Hertfordshire. He was an excellent tennis player, and every time I pass Potters Bar on the train I think of him. Felix only lasted the holiday, but Flush lived to a good old age and died in Daddy's arms. I shall never forget the letter Daddy wrote

to me, as he was obviously heartbroken.

My year in the stables finally came to an end and I had to decide what to do with my life. Music had been an important part of my childhood, and Mummy had a beautiful soprano voice. All her brothers and sisters had wonderful voices, too, as had our grandparents. Strangely, none of us inherited this gift. Given a choice of the arts, I would have loved to be a singer. Every week, Nora and I had gone to Mummy's singing teacher, 'Auntie' Mary Hopley, for lessons at her big, dark house.

When one of us was having a lesson, the other would be banished to the dark and gloomy library, which housed Hans Christian Andersen and Grimm's fairy tales. We dreaded the visits because we had to read those books.

As children, we used to watch plays at Hull Rep, as well as variety shows at the Floral Hall, Hornsea, twice a week throughout the summer. On Sunday afternoons, we would listen to an orchestral concert at the Floral Hall, conducted by one of Mummy's friends, Pattie Hall.

Mummy was an avid theatre-goer who would watch eight West End shows in a

week when Daddy went to London for conferences. With her sweet soprano voice, she was also a member of the local operatic society in Hornsea, often taking the lead in its Gilbert and Sullivan productions. Her sister Ruth, who had a beautiful contralto voice, had actually been offered a job by a professional company, but her parents would not let her go, and she ended up marrying and having a family.

Members of the operatic society would come to our house for rehearsals. We used to slink in and hide under the piano so that we could listen to those wonderful voices—and they *were* wonderful. Hornsea was very lucky, drawing its talents from a wide area.

Nora and I would go round houses selling tickets for their performances and, when the shows were on, we went every night of the week and never tired of them. The last night was always the best, because everyone in the show bought flowers and ornaments and chocolates for the rest of the cast.

Branching out, Mummy started producing plays, first the annual Passion Play for the church at Easter, as well as a concert party that toured local halls under

the name Mrs Fanny Rix And Her Bright Young Things.

There were four main venues; the Floral Hall, in Hornsea, which was always freezing cold because it had glass walls, Granville Court, a hotel that had a ballroom-cum-theatre, parish halls and the Star Cinema.

After making my stage début in *The Windmill Man* at school, I started taking part in Mummy's one-act plays. Naturally, on leaving school, I was in them all the time. Mummy would sing and Nora and I would recite and perform sketches. Brian, too, had shown an aptitude for the theatre, appearing in the Gilbert and Sullivan operetta *The Sorcerer* at a young age and playing lead roles in plays for his prep school. However, he showed no interest in taking to the stage as a career until after he left school. He always intended to be a doctor, although Mummy pushed him towards stage management.

I loved music, but singing was not to be my forte. Having always wanted to go on the stage, I was glad to finish school, which I hated. Bunty, my best friend, always encouraged me to take up acting. She said that when I became a famous actress she would be my secretary, and

when people telephoned, she would say, 'I'm sorry, the Great Rix cannot come to the phone. She is drinking her orange juice.' Teenage jokes! In fact, the Great Rix turned out to be my brother Brian because, by the time I became well known, I had changed my name to Mercier.

Fortunately, my parents also encouraged me to take up acting. They looked around for a drama college away from London where I could live in, eventually finding a beautiful place on the banks of the river at Stratford-upon-Avon, home of our greatest playwright.

For years, there had been moves to start a drama school there and Frank Benson, the great actor-manager, had organised the Stratford Festival. He was getting old and had been involved in a scandal when he ran off to South Africa with his leading lady, who died shortly afterwards. He never returned to Lady Benson, who was by then running a drama school in London.

However, he was asked to become the first director of a drama school in Stratford-upon-Avon, which incensed him as he thought he would be unable to continue running the Stratford Festival. Therefore, Frank Benson turned down the offer. It was

a great tragedy, because he hardly worked again and eventually died in abject poverty in a single room in Holland Park, London. Such were his dire circumstances that he was the only actor-manager to get £100 a year pension on the civil list.

The problem of finding someone to run a drama school continued until the authorities stumbled on Randle Ayrton, who was well known for his performances of Shakespeare at Stratford-upon-Avon and made his name in the title role of *King Lear*. He was generally considered to be the greatest Lear of his generation.

I was the first student to arrive at the newly founded Stratford-upon-Avon College of Drama and, from that moment, was the principal's favourite. There wasn't a lot of talent there, though—many parents simply used the place as a finishing school for their daughters. Girls were often cast as men because, in those early days, there was only one male student—but I had all the best parts.

It was a lovely life. Randle's daughter, Lulu, ran the hostel and we became great friends. Her husband had just died, leaving her with two small children to bring up. But Lulu never believed he had really gone

because, she said, he used to come and talk to her every night!

Eventually, Randle built a beautiful theatre in the grounds of the college, although we staged some of our productions in the garden. *Pan and the Young Shepherd* was performed among the trees, with a lot of girls playing nymphs—it was quite spectacular. We also did *The Comedy of Errors* in the garden, with me playing Adrianna. That was when Donald Wolfit, the great actor-manager who had played Kent to Randle's Lear, was in the audience with the specific aim of finding a new talent for his touring company and afterwards told Randle that he would give me a job when I left.

I was also much encouraged by a review in the *Birmingham Post* of our joint staging of two plays, *The Countess Kathleen*—by the poet W. B. Yeats—and *Pearly Gates*. 'It is usual to mention pupils in terms of promise,' wrote the critic, 'but in the case of Sheila Rix one can speak of definite performance. She has versatility and a confident sense of poise and gesture. It wasn't until I examined the programme afterwards that I realised she played both the Countess Kathleen and the clumsy

aunt in *Pearly Gates.*' That was wonderful, my first review of any importance.

There were two great things that Randle taught me—how to act Shakespeare and how to learn my lines. People used to go to rehearsals with books in their hands, but he would not allow it. I think I would have stayed at drama school for ever if Daddy had not put his foot down and said it was time to put words to music and start acting professionally. The college itself lasted for only a few years. Randle became very ill, couldn't carry on and died shortly afterwards. Those who took over were not nearly as good and eventually it fizzled out. Sadly, the building is now razed to the ground.

2
Home and Away

My first appearance on a professional stage was actually the occasion when Donald Wolfit made his visit to us at the college while appearing at the Shakespeare Memorial Theatre in *Cyrano de Bergerac*. Four of us were asked if we would like to be 'walk-ons'—actors who are seen briefly without speaking any lines. Would we! Along we went and the four of us were dressed up as nuns and admired each other in our wimples, which were very flattering. Then we dressed up as ladies of the court. It was all so exciting appearing with these marvellous actors and actresses and, of course, the great man himself. Donald was superb as Cyrano. I cannot remember the name of his leading lady, but I can recall her face—she was so beautiful. That gave me the first buzz of my theatrical career.

On leaving the Stratford-upon-Avon College of Drama, I was due to tour with Donald Wolfit, but had several months

to fill before that started. I went home for a short spell. Carl Bernard started a repertory company at the old Grand Theatre in Hull, I went to see him and he promised me some parts—good ones, which I was really to enjoy. I was so thrilled to be with him. The excitement of the 'half-hour call' (before the curtain went up) used to make my heart beat wildly. Carl was a very good actor and versatile, which you have to be in rep.

There I was in my own home town actually appearing on stage. My ambitions were endless. I wanted to play Shakespeare more than anything because that had been part of my training. But, apart from 'small parts and tatty pages' with Donald Wolfit shortly afterwards, I was only ever to play Gertrude in *Hamlet* in Huddersfield.

Unfortunately, my luck ran out with Carl after six weeks—he had no more work for me. So I went to London and found myself a room at 29 Oakley Street, Chelsea. Visiting an agent, I was advised that the best way to get started was to pay £30 as a student's fee and get paid thirty shillings (£1.50) a week to work as an assistant stage manager—otherwise known as an ASM—which would also give

me the opportunity to get small acting roles. He found such a place for me in Buckinghamshire and I packed my bags.

Aylesbury was home to one of the many repertory companies that were once the backbone of stage acting in this country. Today, there are few left, but many of our great actors and actresses started in rep. When I arrived in Aylesbury, I sat through a performance of *Young Woodleigh* and was told to get myself a pair of black stockings and a pinny so that I could take the role of a parlour maid the following week.

I returned to the hotel where I was staying and thought hard. The next morning, I got up early and went back to London, leaving a note with the message: 'Sorry I can't stay. You are not up to my standards.' The cheek! Me straight out of drama school. But, when I arrived back in London, there was a telegram from Carl Bernard waiting for me. 'Come back,' it read. 'We have more parts for you.' So back to Hull I went.

In repertory, I always made my own costumes to wear on stage. For *Death Takes a Holiday*, I put together the most beautiful purple gown with a train. Another play we staged was *Little Ladyship* and, although I

don't remember my role, the one line of mine I do recall is, 'Hitler—only a better moustache.' In all, I worked with Carl for three months, performing eight times a week—for the princely sum of £3—and in a new play every week. I had told Carl at the beginning that I was so happy simply acting there that I didn't want any money. 'A labourer is worthy of his hire,' Carl responded.

When not on stage, the company would come *en masse* to our lovely house in Hornsea and Mummy would lay on Sunday teas for them. Unfortunately, Carl had a bulldog called Glamour that was troubled with wind. One day, when he came to lunch, he put the dog under the table. Thank goodness we knew Carl well enough to laugh about it because pungent odours kept rising to assail our nostrils. Glamour? Hardly!

All was to change with the outbreak of war. Our grandparents came to live with us, leaving Hull for what must have been hell, because we were a boisterous lot. On their first night in Hornsea, the sirens went and someone shook a rattle, which was the signal for a gas attack. We sat for hours in our gas masks and

couldn't understand why the dogs didn't die. Grandmother took her mask off first and we all followed suit, then went upstairs to smell peardrops in the air—the same odour as gas. Someone had enjoyed a scented bath and the rest was imagination!

The next day, I phoned Donald Wolfit to ask whether the tour in which I had been contracted to work would be going ahead with its productions, now that we were likely to be bombed off the face of the Earth. He was very cross and said, 'Of course it is—more than ever.' So I set off for London again, eyes constantly skyward, waiting for the raiders who never came.

What I did not know at the time was the tour might well not have gone ahead but for Donald's persistence. Some of the theatre managements in the provinces tried to cancel their contracts with him, fearing that a tour of Shakespeare would be inadvisable in the circumstances and pointing out that the government had indicated theatres might be closed during wartime. Donald simply replied that he intended to proceed with the tour and considered it his duty to present the plays of 'our National Poet' to the British people at such a time.

49

He had, in fact, predicted the likelihood of war five months earlier, while the government insisted that a lasting peace had been won in Munich, from where the Prime Minister, Neville Chamberlain, had brought his famous piece of paper the previous year. Donald sent his wife and children to the Surrey countryside in preparation, claiming to know that Hitler was definitely drawing up battle lines. He knew the German Chancellor, he believed—after all, they shared the same birthday, 20 April, although Donald was thirteen years younger.

So war did break out and the famous actor-manager faced two new problems—holding on to his cast in the light of Parliament's vote in favour of conscription and waiting for his leading lady, Rosalinde Fuller, to return from New York. The second problem looked unlikely to be resolved after her liner failed for a second time to leave port. However, a third attempt was successful and she crossed the Atlantic in time for our opening performance in Brighton. It was a relief that she arrived safely, considering that other ships were being sunk by U-boats.

War or no war, I found myself working

for Donald Wolfit, who had decided to become an actor-manager only two years earlier, creating his Shakespeare Company and taking the Bard's work to the masses both in Britain and overseas.

He was following in the footsteps of a long line of actor-managers. They had proliferated during Victorian times and gained a respect never previously accorded to those on the stage. Many of them were knighted, including Henry Irving (a great Hamlet), Charles Wyndham, John Hare, Johnston Forbes-Robertson (another fine Hamlet) and, perhaps the greatest of them all, Frank Benson (a wonderful Richard II), known to all who worked with him as 'Pa', a reflection of the paternal role this group of thespians played in their companies.

They always took the leading roles and their companies were, in reality, little more than supporting players, but it enabled many aspiring actors to gain a solid grounding in the classics.

It was Frank Benson who did much to establish the original Shakespeare Memorial Theatre at Stratford-upon-Avon, now home to the Royal Shakespeare Company, by performing almost every spring for more

than thirty years and every summer for a decade at the annual Stratford Festival.

Donald Wolfit was one of those actors who made his name at the Shakespeare Memorial Theatre—as well as the Old Vic in London—in the twenties and thirties, and gained critical acclaim for his Hamlet. When he became an actor-manager, which gave him control over his stage career and provided him with a ready supply of leading roles, his own performances were generally praised but his company came in for much criticism.

It could be said that the Donald Wolfit Shakespeare Company was regarded as unfashionable, but it did no one in it any harm and launched the careers of a number of actors, although some already had established stage careers.

Those who worked with him over the years included Lewis Casson, Peter Copley, Ronald Fraser, Joan Greenwood, Raymond Huntley, Peter Jones, Geoffrey Keen, Eric Porter, Frank Thornton, Peter Vaughan, Richard Wattis and even my brother Brian.

Several who acted in Donald's company subsequently became playwrights, such as Harold Pinter, Alun Owen and Ronald

Harwood, his biographer, who became a successful writer after a spell as actor and dresser with Donald. In fact, Ronald's play *The Dresser* was inspired by his years with the company, telling of an actor-manager getting through his last performance of *King Lear* during a provincial stage tour during the war, although it was set before Ronald himself joined the company.

I was, of course, to work with Donald at the start of the war, spending three months learning how to perform Shakespeare. We staged *Hamlet, Othello, The Merchant of Venice, Twelfth Night, The Taming of the Shrew* and a colourful, new production of *Julius Caesar*. I made my début on the tour as a courtier and for much of the time was in small roles or standing by as an understudy, but I did play the widow in *The Taming of the Shrew*.

Despite what I had been taught at drama school, I never bothered to learn lines when I was understudying, I would go to rehearsals with a book in one hand, not believing there would ever be a chance to put them into action. Sometimes there was and, fortunately, I knew the lines.

For *Julius Caesar*, memorable for the coloured togas and the armour designed

by Paul Gibson, extras were brought in for the crowd scenes. In Edinburgh they were medical students, in Cambridge undergraduates, and all the other places had their moments as well. The sad part was that, each week, one member of the company was called up for the war effort, so the cast was constantly depleted and doubling was the order of the day.

Another actress chosen to take part in that tour was Joan Cooper, who had been at Randle Ayrton's drama school with me. We had always played the two female leads there but were now finding our way in the big, wide world. Joan later married Arthur Lowe, forever to be remembered as Leonard Swindley in *Coronation Street* and Captain Mainwaring in the popular television comedy series *Dad's Army*.

Touring with Donald was a very sociable time, with plenty of cocktail parties. In Cambridge, we all got very drunk and Donald—who was not with us—said he would never allow us to go in future unless he was there getting drunk as well! I thought of Donald as a friend as well as an employer. He was a kind man and often came over to see us in Hornsea. However, he could be difficult to work

with and always liked the spotlight firmly on himself. He was very self-centred and, when on stage, everyone else faded into insignificance.

I did once get the better of him. He engaged me at £2 a week, but there was only thirty-five shillings in my pay packet for the first week. So I went to Donald and told him, 'You said £2 to me.' He replied, 'No, no. All the girls get thirty-five shillings.' I brought out my letter of employment and said, 'Here it is in writing.' He was so angry with me!

nice. Next, I was approached by a South
African pilot and chatted to him for about
ten minutes, before he told me that his
cousin had gone to bed and asked me to
help stir his stumps and get him to come
to the party.
We went, but the man who turned

3
Janet

After the tour with Donald Wolfit, which
ended in Norwich during the first week
of December 1939, 1 returned home for
Christmas and a few creature comforts. On
New Year's Eve, one of our RAF officer
friends at a nearby aerodrome phoned to
say that a group of young officers, who
had arrived on their way to another station,
were throwing a party that night and would
my sister and I like to go along with a few
other friends. Mummy and Daddy said yes
we could go—after all, we had been there
many times and always enjoyed ourselves.
I had just washed my hair, which in those
days was a shining auburn, and put on a
green dress. Looking very fetching, Nora
and I went off to the party.

A lot of young men were there, all
getting very merry. I remember they gave
me a glass of what they called Green
Goddess. I don't know if they concocted
the mixture or bought it, but it was very

nice. Next, I was approached by a South African pilot and chatted to him for about ten minutes, before he told me that his cousin had gone to bed and asked me to help stir his stumps and get him to come to the party.

We went, but the man—who turned out to be another nice young South African—would not come to the party. The pilot then asked me to go with him to his room to stoke the fire. This I did and was standing there when, suddenly, I was seized, thrown on the bed and raped—or taken by force, whichever you like to call it.

I screamed and fought and kicked him, and eventually he let me go. I did not think anything drastic had happened because I felt nothing and I was a virgin—determined to keep myself pure for the man I would, I hoped, one day marry. I picked myself up, dusted myself down and, shaking with fright, rejoined the party, before going home.

It was the winter of 1940 and Hornsea was frozen from end to end. When the whole village turned out to skate, play ice hockey and generally have a wonderful time, my boots were too tight. When I took

58

them off, the relief from the pain was great because my feet were frozen too.

Suddenly, each night I started being sick, which went on for a couple of weeks before my mother called the doctor. The first thing he asked me was, 'Have you been misbehaving?' 'No,' I replied, because I didn't think I had been.

I continued to skate and fall on my bottom. You would have thought that alone would have dislodged any unwanted bodies. Anyway, my mother kept giving me funny looks but said nothing. Then came the day when the doctor told me I was to have a baby. I couldn't believe it. How could that night have caused a baby? I had fought him so hard. The doctor told me it was possible to conceive if the sperm only went to the entrance of the vagina and that was what must have happened. I was devastated. What was I going to do?

I had a very strict upbringing and, when I heard of other women having babies out of wedlock, I was shocked. That it could happen to me was completely unthinkable. I had heard of rape as a terrible crime, which indeed it was. Maybe if I had been more worldly wise, I would have done something about it, but in those days

abortion was not something you talked about.

I moved in with my best friend Bunty when her mother was away. She was a true friend to me, but neither of us had any experience of the big, wide world. I must have told half the village that I had missed the curse for three months, and the doctor had said I had catarrh on the stomach, but this was before he told me the dreadful news.

After six weeks with Bunty, I decided to go to London—to get a job in the theatre, as far as my parents were concerned. My favourite cousin drove me down, without any idea that he was driving a runaway. In fact, I went to stay with another cousin in North London, a lovely lady called Sybil, and her husband Basil. However, when I eventually told them what had happened, they promptly phoned my parents and asked them to make the journey to London.

I have a terrible habit of laughing in the face of adversity. When my parents arrived and asked why I hadn't told them and why had I done it, I laughed and said I had done nothing, because in my mind that was the case. They more or

less told me to sort myself out and find a way of living. After they had gone, the tears came, not for myself, but for what I would do to their orderly lives when the story unfolded—which, of course, it did.

I left Sybil and Basil and went to stay with some college friends who lived in Sussex Gardens in Edgware. They were marvellous to me and put up with endless tears because I didn't know what to do.

One of my friends suggested I live with her mother, near Stratford-upon-Avon, which held many happy memories for me from my time at drama school. I took her advice and was also some comfort for her because her family were away fighting. One of them was at Dunkirk and, fortunately, came home alive.

This woman had a lovely garden in which she grew her own asparagus. We had it every day—what a luxury! I stayed there for about a month before my parents came down and gave the old girl some money for my keep, which brought a satisfied smile to her face. Then, my parents told me to push off and find somewhere else to live.

Filled with fear, I set off for Birmingham. Why, I don't know. I knew no one there and arriving in the city was a nightmare.

While waiting anxiously for the baby's birth, my constant thought was, 'Why couldn't my parents do more for me?' After a few nights, I wondered what I was doing in this city and decided to take a train to Nottingham, where I found a small hotel on the outskirts of town and rested my weary bones for a while.

The baby was starting to kick and I was terrified. No one had told me this would happen. In fact, nobody had told me anything. I was friendless and desolate, and completely ignorant.

I found a flat in Nottingham that was furnished, although I had to provide pots and pans—I still have some of the plates to this day. While I was staying there, my father succeeded in tracing the pilot who had raped me. He had approached a very good friend at the Air Ministry called Nobby Clarke, armed only with the man's name, plus the facts that he was South African and had been at that party on New Year's Eve. Not much to go on, but Nobby was determined to find this young man. He succeeded and my father wrote to tell him what had happened. It says something for the man's character that he at least admitted to his crime and came

post-haste to the flat. I asked him if he knew that he had actually had sex with me and he said yes, he did. So I asked why he had not told me.

His reaction to the situation was that we'd better get married. My first thoughts were that I did not want to marry someone who would commit such a deed. Then, I thought that, in spite of the ghastly mess he had landed me in, he really was a nice young man, so I said yes.

However, my parents wouldn't hear of it. I saw their point, which was the same as my initial reaction, and they were right, of course. I had known him for only a few minutes. How could they even contemplate marriage for me to such a man? But I was desperate to keep the baby and marriage was the only answer. Unfortunately, it was not to be.

Mummy then came over to see me with her friend, whom we called Antirrhinum. She took me to see a doctor, then left me again, alone. All the time I had been in the flat, I had not been sleeping and the doctor gave me some pills, but they did no good at all.

As she came to know me, Antirrhinum realised how desperately unhappy and alone

I was. I didn't even have a radio to listen to. Lord knows how I passed the time! The doctor decided that I needed to be part of a family and arranged for me to live with a couple who had a little girl and were in need of a bit of extra money. They were so kind to me.

It was a hot summer and I was feeling the heat. Everything about me was uncomfortable, not just my body, but also my mind. I knew I wasn't going to be allowed to keep the baby, that it had to go for adoption. I rather hoped Antirrhinum would adopt it, because she and I had always been such good friends, but my parents did not think that wise as I would be visiting her home so often.

When the time of the baby's birth came, I was taken to Miss Murray's nursing home in Nottingham, full of fear and trembling, again not knowing what was going to happen. It was pretty nasty. The doctor was at the cinema with her nephew and had to be found. As soon as she came in, she gave me chloroform and I knew no more.

When I came round, they told me that I had given birth to a little girl, but they would not let me see her. I cried for two

days and, eventually, they gave in and brought the baby down to me. She was beautiful and I wondered how I could ever bear to part with her.

The baby's father came to see her and wanted to take her away himself, but that was not allowed. Mummy and Antirrhinum came, but the baby bawled all the time they were there, so I don't think she made a very good impression.

When, three weeks later, it was time to go home, my sister Nora and her boyfriend came to pick me up. When the moment came, I thought my heart would break. How could I part with this precious and beautiful little thing? Nora said she was the most beautiful baby she had ever seen, but she had to be left behind in the nursing home until her adoptive parents could come and pick her up. A good family had been chosen for her, the man being a housemaster at a very famous public school.

So I left her and, going back to Hornsea with Nora, we passed my best friend Bunty, who wrote in her diary that night, 'Sheila's home looking as though her heart has been torn out by the roots.' Two days later, I tried to get the money together to

go and fetch her home, but my parents were watching out for this.

I settled down to life at home and became very ill with cholecystitis. The doctor said I had to go to hospital and have my gall bladder out, but I begged him to leave it until the morning and give me some of his magic medicine, which he did. The next morning, I was much better and stayed in bed for two weeks with a coal fire in the room. Bliss!

After about six months, my baby's adoption papers had to be signed and the stipendiary magistrate came round to witness my signature. I felt awful. 'Stipey', as we called him, was a friend of my parents and, of course, had to be let in on the secret. Secret! Most people seemed to know, but they were all kindness itself. So closed a chapter on my life.

I had named my daughter Karen Mary, but her adoptive parents christened her Monica Janet, although she was always called Janet. Over the next two years, they were very kind and answered all my letters and sent photographs. However, after her second birthday, her father wrote and asked me not to contact them any more

because his wife liked to feel that Janet was her own.

Every time I saw a baby in a pram, I cried and my heart would break, which is why I eventually decided to join the WAAF. It would give me something else to think about, as well as being my way of serving my country during the war.

Years later, a couple of weeks after I started going out with Peter, my husband-to-be, I told him about Janet and he didn't seem to mind. When we married, we did not get the baby we longed for straight away—it took three years. When our son Nigel was born, I wrote to Janet's parents to tell them that I was happy for the first time in fifteen years. I adored my son but still could not get Janet out of my mind.

When I was at the Whitehall Theatre performing in my brother Brian's farces, there were always girls waiting for autographs at the stage door and I used to ask them their names, being absolutely certain that one day Janet would try to contact me. It turned out that she used to haunt the stage door but always missed me.

After I left my final production there, in 1969, I received a letter from Janet—forwarded by the stage door keeper—

that included her address and telephone number, and a photograph of her three young daughters. I was wild with delight and phoned her straight away. She travelled to London the next day and we went to Brian's wife Elspet's for lunch. Talk, talk, talk. I thought we would never stop! It was a wonderful day and I managed to go to Janet's house in Styal, Cheshire, and meet her husband Oliver and the girls.

That night, I told Peter and he was angry. Since I had originally spoken to him about Janet, we had not talked much about her and he probably thought that she would never come into my life again. I was sad, wanting so much for Peter to like her. She came to the house two or three times with Oliver and the family and met Nigel, but always when Peter was not there.

Eventually, I told Nigel the whole sad story because I thought he had a right to know that, if ever he was left alone in the world, he had a half-sister. He said, 'Oh, you mean Mary Poppins.' That was what he called her because she looked just like Julie Andrews!

When Oliver, the most enchanting of men, later retired, he and Janet went to live in Devon, so our meetings became

less frequent. As for the man who raped me, we never brought charges because he was a pilot fighting for his country. In fact, he was a hero who won the Victoria Cross and, a short time later, he was killed.

4
Theatre of War

Following that dreadful time of being raped, having an illegitimate child and losing it to adoptive parents, with my family virtually disowning me, I settled back into my parents' home in Hornsea and had to decide what my contribution to the war effort should be. All my friends were doing something, so I took a crash-course in nursing, joined the Red Cross and landed a job at our local hospital. I enjoyed the work but couldn't stand the smells, because we were given all the nastiest jobs.

There was one boy with empyema who had a hole in his back and I had to dress his wound. I used to soak a piece of cotton wool with *Je Reviens*, put it in my bosom and pull the apron over my nose. I certainly wasn't cut out for nursing. The spirit was willing, but the flesh was weak!

During the summer of 1941, I went to a garden party, where I won a duck and

a boyfriend. In the crowd was a certain wing commander known as 'Wicky', who asked whether he could come and eat the duck with the family. Our home was ever open to the services, so Mummy said yes and romance blossomed over the coming weeks. One night in his car, he said, 'Let's get married.' Sadly, he was posted to Australia, so we were engaged but had no time to wed. I spent a week with him in London, in his flat in Dolphin Square, before he had to travel to Liverpool for his journey Down Under. We tried to get married by proxy after he left, but it didn't work.

Wicky was the first boyfriend who had asked me to marry him. I was devastated about his departure. I even thought about throwing myself under a bus, but I never did, of course. He was away for two years and I wrote to him every day and never went out with another man—faithful, that's me. On Wicky's return, I went to London to see him and stayed for two weeks. He had changed, I had changed and the magic was no longer there, so we parted. A short time afterwards, he married another woman and that lasted just three months. Phew! It might have been me.

By then, I had settled into a wartime job, following my less than successful attempt to be a nurse. I decided to join the WAAF, but failed the medical after being ill with an inflammation of the gall bladder. I was told to go home, lie in the sun and get well, which I did in the garden hammock. By the end of the summer, I was passed fighting fit and on my way to the WAAF. When I went for that second medical, I was thinking to myself, 'I wish I hadn't done this.' I didn't want to go into the Air Force—it suddenly dawned on me that I was going to be away from home, in all sorts of awful places, with awful people, wearing awful clothes. Nevertheless, I was called up and that was that.

The whole family had settled down into its routine for the war. My father's ships were kept busy, Brian was still at school—before going down the mines as a Bevin boy—Nora was a housewife, having married an aeronautical engineer, and Malcolm had become a captain in REME, doing radar work. He had intended to be a solicitor when he left school, but failed his exams eight times, getting tummy trouble every time because of his nerves, which was a shame because he would have been very

good—he was always a good liar!

I shall never forget my first fortnight in the WAAF, at a recruitment centre in Bridgnorth in Shropshire. They used to call me 'Lady La Deda' because, although nobody else seemed to bathe, I would get up at six in the morning and go to the ablutions with my bar of Morny's Sandalwood soap. Whenever I use that brand now, the smell takes me back. We were jabbed, drilled, shouted at, kitted out and endured all the dreadful things one goes through.

My first posting was to Dyce Airport, near Inverness (now Aberdeen Airport), where I was shown to a billet and ordered to share a bed with another girl, as was the routine. Acting a bit above myself, I went post-haste to the WAAF commanding officer and told her it wasn't on, so they gave me the bed of a girl who was on leave. I phoned the transport section with instructions to collect my luggage, which it did, and wondered afterwards how I had the cheek—I did that twice.

After just a week, I was posted further up the east coast of Scotland to Peterhead, a satellite station, which was so cold it felt as if it was near the North Pole, but we

had a lovely, comfortable billet there. The only problem was the maid would put too much salt on the porridge and we couldn't eat it. Unfortunately, they eventually built a WAAF encampment at Peterhead and we had to leave our comfortable billet for terrible Nissen huts.

Our place of work was about two miles away from the station, a little tender that was the radio telephone listening service. I was told to go into signals as an RTO (radio telephone operator) because they needed people with good, clear diction to speak to the pilots. All we did was write down whatever they said. There was an abbreviation for everything, so it wasn't too bad, although the job was simply boring. Very rarely did anything interesting happen.

So cold was it at Peterhead that we kept our great coats on even during the middle of summer. One winter, we had to have provisions dropped by air—mostly sausages.

I was never idle there and staged various plays. My favourite was *Hay Fever*, for which I had a superb cast. And the Argyll and Sutherlanders were stationed there, so we put on a concert for them.

75

They were a pretty rough lot and I decided to recite a poem called 'Ojistoh', about Red Indians. Silly me—they didn't appreciate a bit of dramatic acting at all and clapped and booed me off stage. That was something I never repeated.

Sleeping was a more permanent problem. Our WAAF company decided that the huts we lived in should be mixed, which meant the cooks should live with the plotters, who charted the positions of aircraft and came from a higher educational bracket. That was fine for socialism, but the bellman used to come through our hut at four in the morning to awaken the cooks—and, of course, the rest of us. We also worked night shifts, so sleep was in short supply. There was quite a division between the ranks, with cooks simply the domestic classes, and plotters and others keeping themselves very much to themselves.

One day, when my friend and I were walking to work, the station was bombed. We heard the explosions and, two seconds later, looked up and saw a plane with a swastika very low overhead, so we dived into the nearest ditch as it machine-gunned us. We were both very scared. It is an awesome sight looking up and

seeing swastikas on the underside of the plane after being used to our Air Force rings for so long.

Unhurt, we dashed up to the tender to report to the main station. Such was the chaos that they hadn't even heard about it. This incident reminded me of stories that Mummy and Daddy had told us about the First World War, when they would go into the fields to get away from Zeppelins. I had always had it drummed into me about what it was like and had terrible nightmares over and over again about being bombed and machine-gunned. Once it had actually occurred, the nightmares never happened again.

I spent two winters in Peterhead. After I left, the order was given that no WAAFs should stay there for more than one winter because of the severe climate. I arrived there just a bit too early!

During my stay at Peterhead, Mummy was continuing her plays for the church back in Hornsea. Pretty good they were, too. There was one called *Without the Prince*, the first farce written by Philip King, who came from Beverley—not far from my family's home—and went on to become famous for shows such as *Sailor*

Beware!, which made a star of Peggy Mount.

This one, about farming folk he had observed in the Yorkshire Dales, had a long speech from *Hamlet* that Brian was to deliver as the Stranger. Mummy wrote to me that he didn't know how to handle it. So, because I had performed Hamlet with Donald Wolfit, I took forty-eight hours' leave and went down to coach Brian the only way I knew—how Donald played it.

Going home from Scotland was usually a problem because it was a long journey and a normal, forty-eight-hour pass never left you with much time to spend at home. Peterhead was so off the map that I had to get from there to Aberdeen, before starting a three-part train journey. But I did get to know the waiting-rooms at York, Selby and Hull railway stations very well, and very miserable places they were, too. Still, my coaching must have worked because, shortly afterwards, Brian went along to Donald's dressing-room when his tour of *David Garrick* reached Hull and auditioned for him, performing this piece—which must have been interesting because it was based on his own performance—and reciting a very funny poem called 'Bessie's Boil', by a

Canadian called Robert Service. This poem was one of Brian's set pieces in the concert parties that my mother took to surrounding villages. Donald was obviously impressed because he hired Brian as an assistant stage manager and actor.

Donald had often come to our house for lunch, as a result of my working with him, and was enormously taken with Brian, who had great personality even as a youth. Many times I had said to him, 'One of these days, Brian's going to be with you.' That was the beginning of my brother's life in the theatre.

Although Brian had been taken on by the RAF as a PNB (pilot, navigator, bomb aimer), his service had been deferred for ten months. Therefore, he trooped off with Donald, initially on his 1942 autumn tour, which included the actor-manager's first production of *King Lear*, with Brian playing Kieran the Courtier. This was followed by a season at St James's Theatre, London, during which he acted Sebastian in *Twelfth Night*, and a six-week tour to entertain the troops with ENSA (the Entertainments National Service Association).

After further deferment, Brian infuriated

Donald by not signing another contract with him, opting instead to gain wider experience by going into repertory theatre with the White Rose Players in Harrogate. By the time the war was ready for Brian, demand for pilots was diminishing and he went down the mines as a Bevin Boy, before spending a few months as an RAF medical orderly instructor.

Throughout that time, my contribution to the war effort was continuing unabated. After Peterhead, I was posted to Digby in Lincolnshire, which was a bit nearer home. To get anywhere, I would hitch-hike in those days, with nothing to fear. Now, I wouldn't do anything so hazardous.

We were billeted at Blankney Hall, with about four to a room. The accommodation was quite comfortable, but there were mice that lived in the fireplace and they used to taunt us at night. Once, I left a digestive biscuit beside my bed and was amazed to see it being dragged along the floor by one of our little friends.

While there, I was asked to direct a production of *Quiet Wedding*, but it was a disaster. Arriving at about the third rehearsal, I found everyone sitting reading their scripts, so tried to get them moving

to plot the play, which they didn't want to do. In the theatre, you read the play through, then immediately start to 'move' it. They wanted to go on reading until they knew it and then, at the last minute, put in the movements, which is ridiculous. I couldn't face this, so left the production to someone more experienced in amateur dramatics.

From Digby, I was posted three miles away to an outpost known as the Virgin's Retreat, which was a cluster of Nissen huts housing only women.

It was rather an apt place to be living, since this was about the time my intended husband returned from Australia. That, of course, never worked out, but I threw myself into a new job, on the DF homer, which was a bit scary at first.

Aircraft used to call when they were lost and I had to give them their course home. At night, sitting there with headphones on, I would hear a pilot calling—and nobody else but I would hear. This turned out to be a great job. I felt as if I was doing something worthwhile and many a pilot phoned later to say thank you.

Next, I went a short distance away to Coleby, where someone stole my bicycle.

That was a terrible loss because I used to go for long bike rides in my spare time. I didn't stay there long and was posted to Hutton Cranswick, between Beverley and Driffield in Yorkshire. What joy! I could get home every week, sometimes only for the day, but my hitching habit made those miles melt away and I was thoroughly happy. I even went on the pillion of a motorbike once.

One day, when I was home on a sleeping-out pass, I attended a ball at the Floral Hall in Hornsea. The Free French of General Leclerc's desert army were there, training before returning overseas. I watched a tall, dark, bearded, handsome man step on to the stage and thought, 'That's the man for me.' We met and danced, he came back to my parents' house and we talked all night. He was the most devastatingly charming man I had ever met, and we fell in love hook, line and sinker.

It's wonderful to be courted by a Frenchman. They have a way with women that is spell-binding. At least mine had! We then went to a dance at Wassand Hall, headquarters of Leclerc's army. General De Gaulle and General Leclerc were both there. It was a night I shall never forget.

Minstrels played in the gallery and we were still dancing on the grass by the lake in the morning.

The Desert Rats had been in a terrible state when they arrived in Britain. They had not worn clean clothes for weeks and all looked as if they had been through the mud, although they had actually been through the sands, chasing the Germans out of North Africa in the El Alamein campaign. Charles, who was in the tank regiment, would never speak about that. Their clothes stank to high heaven, but the Americans rekitted the soldiers and they all came out looking nice and clean.

My Desert Rat and I became engaged weeks after our first meeting. I went to Hull to see the stipendiary magistrate to get permission to marry Charles in a civil ceremony. By the time permission came, our own personal D-Day had arrived and Charles was gone, having made me promise to get a commission because it was not really *comme il faut* for a well brought-up young lady to be in the ranks.

So I put in for officer status and went down to London for my interview before a commission board, where I had the most terrible shock. I was walking down

the street looking for York House, where the board was being held, and I had my overnight bag in one hand and gas mask in the other. Then, my eyes met those of a wing officer and I didn't have a hand with which to salute her. I thought, 'Oh, Christ! I bet she'll be on the board.' When I arrived, there she was. What a shock! 'I don't suppose you were expecting to see me on the board?' she asked. 'Oh, yes, ma'am,' I replied, 'I bet myself my bottom dollar I would.' That made all of the board laugh and I passed. I had applied for a commission in equipment because it was the only opening there was, but they asked if I would rather be an adjutant and I told them I certainly would.

Charles and I never did marry. I wrote to him every day for a long time, but was finally sent to a station where there were a lot of fun people and didn't think about him very often. He later wrote to me saying that we would be married on 17 April 1944, but I was having a bit of a fling with a pilot at the time, so I wired back to say that I couldn't get leave. Silly me! It was only a fling, but I never saw Charles again or heard from him until years later. My father

was furious with me for telling him not to come!

After getting through the interview board and becoming an officer, I moved to the Officer Cadets Training Unit, in Windermere, of all the lovely places, getting a commission as Charles had told me to do. It was winter and beautiful, with snow on the ground. We square-bashed in the snow and had to take turns to do the drilling, which came easy to me. But the lectures we sat through—there was so much to remember. Living conditions were pretty grim, with six cadets to a room, in three bunk beds, and one loo between about thirty of us. It was chaos in the morning. At least the dining-room wasn't so bad and we did learn to pass the port! I remember riding a horse a lot around the countryside and going to a hotel for a dinner of roast duck. It was called the Boar's Head, but we called it the Whore's Bed!

Following Windermere, I went to Hereford on a short administration course so that I could be an assistant adjutant. I passed and was sent to my first posting as an officer, at RAF Boulmer in Northumberland, a satellite station where I was to be admin commanding officer and

adjutant. I had a very good orderly room corporal who did all my work for me and I just signed everything. I got by, but desk work is not really for me. One advantage of being based there was that it was by the sea and the local fishermen used to sell us the most delicious lobsters for 2s 6d (12½p) each. I also managed to go up in an aeroplane. When the orderly room girls all wanted to fly, the commanding officer said I should set an example. Despite telling him that nothing would get me up in a plane, he said it was an order. 'Okay,' I replied, 'but you hold my hand.' We went up, I loved it and wanted more.

So I went over to the main station and pestered the commanding officer to let me go up in a Miles Magister, a two-seater. I went and the CO told the pilot to give me hell, which he did. We looped the loop, waggled the wings and shot up the station. They expected me to get down looking green, but I hopped out smiling. I was hooked on flying for ever.

Whenever I wanted to go to another station for a party or any other reason, I just asked for a plane—and got one. The CO said they might as well practise taking

me around instead of just flying in the sky doing nothing!

From there, I went further north, to the main station at Eshott, again in Northumberland, before being posted to Llanbedr in North Wales, where I found a boyfriend, the squadron leader, who played the piano by ear. We had many a bawdy sing-song. Unfortunately, he had a passion for pickled onions and ate several every day, so I learned to eat them too, out of self-defence. He also said he drove better when he was drunk, and I had many hairy moments when we used to travel back from an evening out.

Next, I went to Middleton St George, near Darlington, which is now Teesside Airport, and learned how to play Liar Dice. It was a new game to me, where you have to say what is in front of you and, if the other players correctly guess whether you are lying or not, have to pay a forfeit.

There was also a fellow-actor there, Ronnie Marsh, who was entertainments officer, so we got together and performed Noël Coward's *Private Lives*. We had a really good cast and I remember having a beautiful negligée made in Hornsea

specially for the play. Ronnie wasn't a beautiful man, but was a jolly good actor and made a super Elyot.

He was also a squadron leader pilot, who fourteen months after the war ended was to fly me down to Nottingham to be demobbed. This was the last of my free airlifts. I had already heard the news that war was ending before it happened, while I was at Eshott, and celebrated two nights running—before and after! In those days, gin and whisky were so cheap—just a shilling each—and a glass of beer was only three old pence.

I had always wanted to go down to where all the action was, but it was not to be. Throughout the war I had remained in Fighter Command 13 group and the nearest I got to the big stations where the bombers went from was during my stay in Digby.

Coming out of the WAAF in June 1946, I went to Esher, in Surrey, to look after one of my girlfriends—a friend of my former fiancé Wing Commander 'Wicky'—who was married to a Navy captain. She was due to have a baby at home and needed someone to run the house for her. I had no idea how to run a

house, though, because we had always had maids at home.

I was a terrible cook, except for steaks and Madeira cake. At home, I had always been allowed to cook the steak because it was reckoned the maids did not know how. I also knew how to make jam tarts, but had never actually cooked a meal. Often queuing for hours to get food for my friend, I once bought a rabbit, didn't know how to cook it and stood over the stove for three hours until it was ready. The baby was also late arriving, but when it did I was allowed to go in and watch. I've never seen anything so moving in my life and the tears poured down my cheeks. The little girl was called Amanda and I became her godmother.

While I was staying so close to London, I took the opportunity to go into the city and join Reunion Theatre, a company formed by Nigel Patrick and Oscar Quitak for actors who had been in the services. The idea was to put on several fifteen-minute pieces so that producers and directors could see what talent was on offer. I played a cockney girl in *Nine to Six* and, afterwards, was asked if I would audition for a television production of

Exercise Bowler, a play that was running at the Scala Theatre in London.

The part was that of a middle-aged Yorkshirewoman and I got it. It was amazing, really, because I was playing much older than myself and there were hundreds of others of the right age going for it. Nevertheless, I wore a wig and we rehearsed for three weeks, performed the play live on the BBC and repeated it three weeks later. For all that, I was paid the princely sum of twenty-one guineas.

After the first rehearsal, the director came over and told me to bring my performance down by half. I was too used to the theatre and played to the gallery. He never gave me another 'note' until the day of the first performance and I thought he had given up on me. Then, he came and said that it was so perfect that he didn't want to change one little thing. But it was terribly frightening since television was something new to me. It was also live, which meant that if I made a mistake there was nothing I could do about it. Both my brothers, Malcolm and Brian, were amateur radio hams and rigged up a wireless so that they could hear the sound from the television production.

Campbell Singer, John Warner and Gillian Maude starred in the play on television, although they did not appear on the subsequent tour of Germany, entertaining British troops. The rest of the cast for the tour were from the Combined Services Entertainment Unit.

Meredith Edwards, a Welsh actor with a voice like Richard Burton, who still does voice-overs for documentaries, played my husband on the tour, and another member of the cast was the late Alan Badel. He was a marvellous actor and wicked, doing anything to send me up. During the show, he had to show me a photograph and once produced one of three nude men. Why it seemed funny I don't know—we've all seen pictures of nude men—but I just fell about.

The tour was not really too serious because it was performed only for British soldiers, not to paying customers, so if we giggled a bit it hardly mattered. The morale of the troops was quite high because they were out there just marking time until their return home. We went to so many beautiful places—Hamburg twice, Flensburg, Lüneberg, Celle, Badsaltsuflin, Badoinhausen, Iselon, Düsseldorf, Berlin

and many others. You could buy anything for cigarettes in those days and the NAAFI centres were full of perfumes and other goodies.

There was also the chance to ride during the tour, and my friend Christine Russell was a superb horsewoman and taught me a lot. Once, in Iselon, they put me on a racehorse called Captain, but without telling me it was a racehorse! That horse had complete charge of me and did exactly what he wanted, which was not always what I wanted. But I survived and didn't lose my nerve, as I thought I would.

Parties, too, were everlasting. Because we had nothing much to do all day, we partied at night. I once got very drunk on a German gin called Steinhagen. My word it was lethal! I learned a lesson there and stuck to what I knew. While in Berlin, we went to the East to see where Hitler had died. That was an eerie feeling and we were glad to get back to our side of the fence. When I knew I was going to Germany, I was pleased because I thought I would come home speaking German. But not a bit of it—everyone spoke English. All I learned was 'Can I have a glass of water/beer, please?', 'Number twenty-two'

(the number of my room in Düsseldorf), and 'Please' and 'Thank you'.

Düsseldorf and Berlin were the most devastated cities after the war. Where there was a building, it would be only one storey high. I never saw any food shops and wondered what people lived on. I bought switches and curls for my hair, all for cigarettes or soap powder, and lots of beautiful glasses and exquisite little coffee cups, and a large crate of champagne.

When we were due to go home, we went from Cuxhaven to Hull, my home port. It was the coldest winter on record, with the rivers freezing over, very little heating and bedrooms like ice. The crossing was bad, with everyone being sick in their cabins—except me, that is. I spent my time eating in the dining-room!

On arriving in Hull, I discovered that my crate of champagne had been stolen, but I had plenty to declare, all piled into old school trunks. The customs officers asked if I was any relation to old Robert Rix and, of course, I said that he had been my grandfather, so they waved me on. I never had to declare any of it and still have those coffee cups and glasses!

This was the start of the coldest winter

in Britain, beginning in late 1946 and running well into the following year. Food and fuel were scarce, electricity was turned off at all sorts of odd hours, and we had to put all our clothes on and huddle together to get warm. We were all right at home because my mother was a skilled provider and always had something up her sleeve to make life more bearable. I stayed long enough to rest and distribute perfume to all my family and friends. That made me very popular because there was none over here.

Looking for work, I took advantage of my grandfather's connection with Arthur Rank many years earlier and wrote to Rank's son with the hope of getting a break in films. I was invited to his Park Lane offices in London, where his right-hand man welcomed me. He suggested that I should write in and they would let me know should any suitable roles come up. However, I had no need to do so as theatre work soon came flooding in.

5
Twice Nightly

In *The Stage,* which is the actors' paper, there was an advertisement for someone to take the role of Mrs Ginnocci with Arthur Lucan and Kitty McShane, who had been playing Old Mother Riley and Her Daughter Kitty for more than thirty years. It was an act they developed in Ireland, where they had met and married, and then taken around the world. They had even made a string of Old Mother Riley films in the thirties and forties. Requesting an audition, I was invited to see the stage show, and the laughter was like a wall falling down. I was mystified because I never cracked a smile once.

They gave me the job and I prepared for the tour, which was starting in Boscombe, on the South Coast, and included a performance at the Finsbury Park Empire. Once rehearsals began, I knew I was in for trouble. Arthur loved to send me up and I only had to look into those wicked blue

eyes to go into paroxysms of laughter. I just used to laugh my way through the whole show every night. It made me very nervous because I knew it was going to happen, so I tried desperately to prevent it. Inevitably, I failed. This couldn't go on, so at the end of the month they had had enough and I most certainly had, so we parted company. It was a good lesson and I learned a lot, although it was funny that Arthur should make me laugh so much on the stage but not watching from an audience.

The scenes between Kitty and Arthur off stage are notorious. She was awful to him, treating him like a dog. One night, at Chelsea Palace, there was a famous comedian in the audience who came up on the stage to gag around with Arthur. Kitty marched on and shouted 'Off!' to Arthur. She didn't like the fact that he was getting so many laughs.

There was perpetual bickering between them and Arthur was very unhappy. They later split up, with Bela Lugosi starring alongside Arthur in his last screen appearance, the 1952 film *Mother Riley Meets the Vampire*, but no Kitty. Two years later, during a tour of *Old Mother Riley Goes to Paris*, Arthur died in the wings at

the Tivoli Theatre, Hull, my home town.

After my short time with those music hall legends, I went back to the pages of *The Stage* and found director Philip Stainton advertising for a cast in Warrington, Cheshire. Philip, who later acted in London's West End, gave me leading lady roles. I couldn't believe it—I had landed everything I had gone for so far.

We began a twice-nightly season at the Theatre Royal, Warrington, starting with *The Man Who Came to Dinner*. Philip played the lead and directed us from his wheelchair, which was part of the play because his character had a broken leg. He was a fantastic director, with a super cast who worked really hard. Philip taught me everything and I owe a lot to him for his direction and tuition.

I was living in digs that, compared with my WAAF years, were quite comfortable. I had a nice, big room with a double bed, but the food was awful. The landlady once bought a duck to give us a treat and boiled it. Needless to say, it tasted foul.

Also, every Sunday, I had the most dreadful, bilious attack and the trots. Fortunately, it was on our day off. In the end, I became so desperate that I

went to a specialist, who asked me what conditions I was living in. It turned out that the landlady's habit of leaving food on the table was responsible for my Sunday attacks. Flies would get to the food and I was being poisoned by them.

Another problem from which I suffered was verrucas on the heel and ball of my foot. I went to the chiropodist twice a week and she burned them out. I was in agony for six months. In the end, she could do no more for me, sent me to a skin specialist and, two weeks later, they were gone, as if by magic.

We finished the season at Warrington, went home for Christmas and returned to the Theatre Royal for the New Year, devils for punishment.

But I was getting wonderful parts to play—both character and straight—and revelled in it. The plays included *Smiling Through* and *East Lynne,* which my brother Brian came to see. He was on his way to being demobbed in Blackpool and stayed overnight in Warrington.

One play, *This is My Life,* was the story of a nurse who falls in love with a doctor very much younger than herself. They had a very passionate love scene in the

middle, during which the mantelpiece at the back of the set fell down one night. We carried on as if nothing had happened and the assistant stage manager responsible for the props said it was because there were real flowers on stage, which is considered unlucky in the theatre.

That incident would probably have been more understandable in another play we did, *The Poltergeist*. Things were moving across the stage all the time, but my biggest problem was the leading man, Robert Marshall, who had the same effect on me as Arthur Lucan. He had a wicked look in his eye and, over the course of two years, we spent all our time laughing.

With the season finished, again I went home to Hornsea to rest and gather my strength. Then, I was asked to go to Bexhill, in East Sussex, where Campbell Singer—who had been in the TV production of *Exercise Bowler* with me—was running a repertory company with Pat Nye, an actress from Reunion Theatre. There, I worked with actors such as Andrew Sachs, who had been born in Germany and came over here shortly before the war. Now, of course, he's famous as Manuel, the bumbling Spanish waiter in

Fawlty Towers, but in those days he was just an assistant stage manager starting out on his career. He was so good in the parts he played.

I also had some lovely roles during my six weeks on the South Coast, in productions such as *Thunder Rock,* a very powerful play by American dramatist Robert Ardrey, who as a scientist is also known for his theory of 'the territorial imperative'. First performed at the beginning of the Second World War, the play was very strong on allegory, telling the story of a lighthouse keeper's encounters with the spirits of shipwrecked travellers and how they rekindle his fighting spirit. Heavy stuff!

The set-up in Bexhill was much more professional than it had been in Warrington. However, my friends from Warrington—including Robert Marshall—were starting a theatre in Tonbridge, Kent, and begged me to go there. So it was off for another season of rep, playing leads, character parts and, occasionally, juveniles.

Some of the plays we staged we had already performed in Warrington, so I enjoyed them all over again. That was a wonderful period of my life, working with

some wonderful people.

The cast rented a cottage at Pembury, with me acting as housekeeper, a role in which I was typecast throughout my career in rep. To be honest, though, I was always the one who volunteered, so I cannot complain.

I spent only a few months in Tonbridge because I had to go to the rescue of my brother Brian. He had decided on a career as an actor-manager after leaving the RAF, influenced by his time with Donald Wolfit—and the fact that there were very few opportunities for actors coming out of the forces a couple of years after the war. He also liked the idea of being his own boss. So Brian started hunting around for a theatre and found the King's Hall in Ilkley, West Yorkshire, which was not really a theatre but would nevertheless do the job.

His next problem was finding a leading lady for his season there and he had asked me before I went to Tonbridge. However, I thought better of working for my brother and, indeed, had no need to do so. Unfortunately, the actress he eventually found proved to be disastrous and, after three or four weeks, Brian sent out an SOS

101

and I duly travelled north.

Ilkley is a beautiful place to live, but the audiences were not very big and the season was not a great financial success—in fact, Brian lost £3,000 after stumping up £1,000, of which £900 was borrowed from our father and Uncle Bertie. However, we all had a good time, and Brian was very grateful to me and more than pleased with my performances.

One of our best productions was *The Eagle Has Two Heads*, with beautiful, authentic costumes borrowed from a Mrs Hill, who lived in Ilkley. Brian had a fantastic set designer and an excellent stage manager, so the plays were off to a good start before the actors even got on the stage. Peter Lait, the stage manager, used to go round big houses begging, stealing or borrowing furniture. We did *Portrait in Black* with a black set and white furniture. It sounds unbelievable, but it was so good. As I had done through all my repertory career, I made a dress or dresses for the next production every Sunday, so I was kept busy.

Nine of us rented a large house and I was, of course, the housekeeper, hiring a wonderful 'daily' woman who came to

clean and cook lunch for us. This was a very wise move on my part and certainly made life easier for all of us.

There was still food rationing in those post-war days, but our 'daily' could make a lovely pie out of a tin of corned beef. Every Thursday, it was tripe for those who liked it and sausages for those who didn't. I love tripe with onions and white sauce. So does Brian and, when we visited Mummy, she often gave it to us as a treat. I never have it now, though, because my late husband, Peter, always hated it—without even having tested it.

Our time at Ilkley came to an end and, reluctantly, we closed ranks and set off for Bridlington. The chance of another season was a relief to Brian, who had just lost a small fortune, but we were not given the best possible start. We went to the seaside resort of Bridlington, which is on the East Yorkshire coast, about fourteen miles north of Hornsea, in November 1948, just as winter was setting in and gales were lashing the seafront. This meant we could not perform at the Spa Theatre, which was where summer seasons were enjoyed, but had to present our winter productions inland, at the Grand Pavilion.

We successfully mounted a pantomime, *Babes in the Wood,* and performed some of the same plays we had done in Ilkley.

One of them was *The Eagle Has Two Heads,* with Brian playing the intruder, and the two of us were supposed to be lovers. As brother and sister, we had a problem. In this play, we had to kiss, but we simply couldn't. In the end, we cut out the kiss! We did play husband and wife many times, but we never actually embraced. We both agreed on that.

Brian decided to form a second repertory company, at the Hippodrome in Margate, Kent, and wanted someone he could trust to be down there. That turned out to be me and the first play I did there was *Jupiter Laughs,* as a harridan of a matron.

In the cast, as a doctor, was a tall, dark handsome man called Peter Mercier, who was to become my husband. I had never before met anyone with such charisma. I fell head-over-heels in love with him but, sadly, he was shipped off to Bridlington, so romance never had a chance to blossom.

I worked hard that season, and we had a wonderful cast and were very successful. William Franklyn, later to become famous for the Schweppes TV

commercials ('Scchh! You know who!'), was with us and gave an excellent performance in a play called *French for Love.*

My sister, Nora, a very good amateur actress, joined the company in Margate for a couple of weeks and later appeared for Brian in *When We are Married* in Bridlington. If he needed someone to fill a tricky part, he would often send for Nora. Better the devil you know! She had, of course, married instead of going to drama school.

We had wonderful weather that year. I remember bathing in the sea at Margate at Easter and the sun continued throughout the summer. My parents and I went on holiday to Paris, where it was so hot that the pavements burned our feet. However, we need not have bothered to go abroad—the weather was even better back home.

Brian had by now become engaged to the actress Elspet Gray, whom he auditioned for the season at Margate but immediately shipped up to Bridlington, and they were preparing for their wedding, in August 1949.

We had been busy in our usual way,

making lovely clothes for the big day. I still have my dress in the loft, but I was slim then and don't suppose it would even go over my head now! The wedding reception, at the family home in Hornsea, spilled out into the garden and sunshine. I was wearing new shoes but, as is my wont, kicked them off, preferring to potter around in stockinged feet. Soon, there were shoes everywhere—everyone dispensing with theirs in the heat.

Shortly afterwards, I started a spring season at Margate. It was great fun and even some of the same people were with me, as well as Elspet's sister Rhoda Gray, who was scenic artist. The season only lasted a few weeks because they wanted too much money from Brian to rent the theatre throughout the summer, so I rejoined the Bridlington company at the Spa Theatre, to which it had moved for the summer season. That caused Brian a few problems because he had replaced me with another leading lady, Jane Meredith. I wanted to return and, eventually, she volunteered to leave, although that was not a happy time. Brian remembers me and Jane clashing, with him left floundering in the middle.

Following his wedding, my relationship

with Brian began to change anyway. I had always been the loving sister who did everything I could for her younger brother In rep together, we shared a house and I became not only housekeeper but, in some ways, a mother figure to him.

I gradually had to learn that I could no longer organise the domestic side of Brian's life. Little matters, such as who would make the sandwiches for him on matinée days, began to cause slight friction between me and Elspet. Brian now had a wife to make him sandwiches.

On another front, my second season in Bridlington was exceedingly happy. Peter, the man I had met in Margate and with whom I had fallen in love, was there. So began the romance of my life, and we were to be together for forty-two years.

The company then moved back to the Grand Pavilion, Bridlington, continuing to work there while Brian and Elspet opened in London with *Reluctant Heroes*, a very funny play about National Service recruits, which they had tried out with great success in Bridlington.

Written by Colin Morris, it had been doing the rounds for four years, but no one realised its potential until Brian put

it on at the Spa Theatre in July 1949 and broke box-office records. Now, he was preparing to take it on a seven-month tour, followed by a run at the Whitehall Theatre in London. It stayed there for a remarkable four years and, in 1951, was made into a film that became the biggest hit of the year in British cinemas. Brian also performed an excerpt on television, the first stage production to be screened from a theatre. Thus began Brian's long run on television.

Betty Impey, who had played one of the ATS girls in the original production of *Reluctant Heroes* in Bridlington, thought that Brian would not want her in the West End production. However, Peter and I persuaded her otherwise. That led to Betty meeting John Chapman, who acted in Brian's shows at the Whitehall Theatre and was also to write some of the successful farces performed there. They married and have four sons.

In Bridlington, I also starred in *The Blind Goddess*, opposite Basil Radford, recreating his original London success as Sir John Dering in the play. Basil was famous in the cinema for the Charters and Caldicott comedy-thrillers that cast him

and Naunton Wayne as two Englishmen abroad, first seen in Alfred Hitchcock's *The Lady Vanishes*. He died of a heart attack just a couple of years later, still only in his fifties. Basil typified the English stereotype, a man more interested in cricket than the dramas going on around him, and was a highly respected comedy actor.

Once the Bridlington season was over, we went to London to stay with Peter's mother. Peter then landed the part of a pirate and Captain Hook's understudy in *Peter Pan*, opening at the old Scala Theatre, with Margaret Lockwood in the title role. She was, in fact, a cousin of Betty Lait, one of the cast from Bridlington, who at one time had money troubles and was certainly looked after by Margaret, who was very kind to her. Of course, during the forties, Margaret had become one of Britain's biggest film stars, particularly memorable in *The Wicked Lady*, and was known for her trademark beauty spot painted high on her left cheek. She seemed a bit distant, perhaps because of the fame that had suddenly come to her. In fact, in her later years, Margaret became a recluse and was hardly seen

outside her Surrey home, right up until her death.

Peter was due to tour in *Peter Pan*, although Margaret appeared only in the Scala production. But first he came up to Hornsea and said he thought we should get married and asked if I would like to. Would I like to!? I had waited nearly two years for this. My parents did not really approve of my marrying Peter and refused to help me with money towards buying a wedding dress. I had lived with him for two years, so I should have known him. I went into Hull, bought some pink material and made my own dress, which was fine. We obtained a special licence and had our wedding set for fifteen days later, at 9 am on 26 March 1951—Easter Monday—at the beautiful church in Hornsea. Peter, who was performing that week in Bradford on the tour of *Peter Pan*, came up to Hull on the Sunday with his best man, Michael Peake, who was also in the cast, and they both hit the whisky bottle.

When the big day came, I could not remember on which side of Daddy I had to walk up the aisle and we collapsed in giggles, which was very unseemly. After the ceremony, we went home to a sort

of reception. There were only best friends there because we had not sent out any invitations.

My father was angry because he thought we should have waited and had a 'bit of a do'. 'And think of all the wedding presents you will miss out on,' he said. 'Think of all the money we are saving you,' I said. 'You can give that to us instead.' Of course, he never did and we started married life on £10 a week and an overdraft.

Peter was back on stage in Bradford that night, so we booked into a Bradford hotel for our 'honeymoon' with our half-whippet, half-Labrador, Prince, on a cold and snowy day. However, we were soon sent packing when I spilled hot water on the eiderdown of the bed and the owners insisted the stain had been caused by the dog.

We then found some theatrical digs, where Prince was welcome, and had a super week. The two women who ran the digs gave us a party and a lot of the *Peter Pan* cast came along.

Peter finished the tour, we returned to London and Clement Lister offered both of us a joint contract at Huddersfield Rep, where he was about to direct. He had been

leading man at Bridlington and most of the cast were friends of ours, people we had worked with before, and Elspet's sister, Rhoda, was scenic artist. Alas, Rhoda died of cancer a few years ago, which was very sad. She was such an enchanting girl and great friends with Elspet, something that doesn't always happen in a family. She has been greatly missed.

Margaret Jackson was another buddy of mine in the cast. We had been together in Reunion Theatre and she was in Huddersfield with her husband, Michael Peake—who, of course, had been best man at our wedding.

Clement Lister was a good actor and director, but he later left the theatre to enter a monastery, before getting involved in research on the Loch Ness Monster and writing novels. I was tickled to death the day I picked up his first best-seller, *Hardacre*, about young people travelling by road and ending up in Bridlington. It was all about the East Riding of Yorkshire and was followed by *Hardacre's Luck* and more stories. When he died, his wife took over writing the novels.

Maurice Durant, who had also been in Bridlington with us, was one of the

leading men in Huddersfield, and what a superb actor he was. Later, he gave up the theatre to retire to the country. Lord knows why—he was a natural. He married Mary Howard, who was also in the cast at Huddersfield, and we all still get together very occasionally. When we do, the years seem to disappear and it's as if we had met only the previous week.

That season, we lived with a Mrs North, who was very careful with her heating. Peter and I used to go into the woods and collect logs to burn on the fire in the front room on Sundays, when we were polishing up our lines for the following week's performances.

For the next season, we found a flat in Kirkburton, five miles out of Huddersfield. It was attached to a workmen's café and the couple who ran it would put their delicious food in our oven for when we arrived home from rehearsals.

That year, we had a star in the cast every alternate week, which could be fun or not, depending on who it was. Dinah Sheridan was one who was, appearing in *Sweet Aloes*—a play actually written by the actress Joyce Carey. Dinah came to our flat a lot and walked in the countryside

with us. During her walks with us, she would talk about her unhappy married life to actor Jimmy Hanley.

He was himself a very successful film star, best known at that time for his role in the Huggetts comedies, with Jack Warner and Kathleen Harrison, which were later turned into a long-running radio serial called *Meet the Huggetts*. He went on to present *Jim's Inn*, which was an ITV advertising magazine—a programme sponsored by advertisers, something peculiar to the early days of commercial television in this country—with his second wife, Margaret Avery. He and Dinah had a daughter, Jenny, who also became an actress, appearing on television in *Emmerdale Farm* and as a presenter of the children's programme *Magpie*, and son Jeremy, who became a Conservative MP and party chairman.

Dinah had been the first actress to appear in the BBC's regular television broadcasts, when she appeared in *Picture Page* in 1936, and her film career was to end only after making the charming British comedy *Genevieve*. She decided to go into retirement upon her marriage to Rank Organisation executive John Davis, which

ended in divorce. A third marriage, to John Merivale, was more successful, but lasted only briefly until his death. Dinah had by then popped up in a couple more films, most memorably as the mother in *The Railway Children*, and has more recently been seen on television in series such as *Don't Wait Up*. She has remained a good friend.

Leslie French, at that time famous for his role in *Charley's Aunt*, came to Huddersfield for that very production, and Kay Kendall came for the Somerset Maugham play *The Letter*. Kay had been appearing in films from the age of seventeen, but was about to make perhaps her best remembered appearance, in *Genevieve*, alongside Dinah Sheridan, Kenneth More and John Gregson, in the tale of two couples engaging in a bit of friendly rivalry in the London-Brighton veteran car rally. In 1957, Kay married Rex Harrison, but died just two years later from leukaemia.

On the Thursday before her week in Huddersfield, she told our director that she couldn't learn *The Letter* and to give her role to the leading lady, who was me. 'If she can't learn it in all the time she's

had, I can't learn it in three days,' I said. 'Get stuffed!' So everything changed. Kay had been performing in *Pygmalion* in Halifax, so that's what we had to learn. Maurice Durant played Higgins and was DLP—dead-letter perfect—as well as being excellent, and I played Mrs Higgins. That was the week our beloved dog Prince died and I didn't need any make-up—my eyes were closed up with weeping.

Monocled Ralph Lynn, known as the master of aristocratic silly-ass types in films and stage farces, also came to Huddersfield. He had been particularly successful in partnership with Tom Walls during the twenties and thirties in farces such as *Rookery Nook* and *Plunder* on stage at the Aldwych Theatre and in films for British and Dominions Studios. This was the period of Ben Travers' and Vernon Sylvaine's very English farces, when trousers were dropped but there was no sexual connotation, unlike in the form's French predecessors.

The duo had long since split up—Tom had, in fact, died a couple of years earlier—and Ralph was no longer making films. However, he had re-established himself in stage farces with Robertson

Hare, who had appeared with him at the Aldwych on stage and in the cinema many years earlier, and he was still a name that would sell tickets at the theatre box office.

So Ralph arrived to do a new play and it was hysteria time. He didn't know a line and we literally had to feed the words into his mouth, say goodbye so that he would leave the stage at the right moment and say hello when he was due to come on.

He might have had difficulty learning his lines, but my goodness how he could make a speech! After the show, he stepped forward and, for half-an-hour every night, he had us in stitches. It was all completely off the top of his head. A brilliant man.

Ralph loved to come to Kirkburton because we gave him boiled eggs for tea and he enjoyed anything simple. We also had a television set. It had only a nine-inch screen, but he was glued to it and loved watching children's programmes, especially *Muffin the Mule*, which was presented by Annette Mills, the elder sister of actor John Mills.

Other stars who graced us with their presence included thirties film star Henry Kendall, Lupino Lane, Donald Houston

(who had become famous as the star of his first film, *The Blue Lagoon*, alongside Jean Simmons) and Jean Kent, the *femme fatale* of the British screen, who took the lead in *The Lady's Not for Burning* in Huddersfield. They were treated like royalty by the rest of the cast and we left them to themselves until they approached us.

Another actress who appeared with us in Huddersfield was Prunella Scales, then in the early years of her career. She was just a jolly little girl then, appearing in *Pride and Prejudice*. Of course, she later became famous on television as Sybil Fawlty in *Fawlty Towers* and Sarah in *After Henry*, although she has shown herself to be a dab hand at playing Queen Victoria on stage and television in her own, one-woman show. She is, of course, married to actor Timothy West.

Maurice Browning, who had suffered from polio a few years earlier and was severely disabled, was our director for that season in Huddersfield. The pluck of the man—he even went on stage and played the most exciting parts. Cassius, our new puppy, always barked at him. He couldn't bear anybody who wasn't

completely normal or who had a peculiar hat on, such as a policeman.

Peter and I were on a joint contract at £24 a week, so we had been able to save and buy a magnificent car, a twenty-year-old Austin Seven, which cost us £90. That was before spending £300 on repairs and eventually selling it for £15 because we couldn't afford to insure and tax it. No wonder after that! We called the car Flook. Two days after our dog Prince's death, we went out to buy Cassius, who had a lean and hungry look. He used to sit in the front seat of our new car, lording it over everyone.

Poor Cassius. He had a bad start in life because he had hard pad and then suffered double-pneumonia. Luckily for him, Peter went ill that week with jaundice, so they were patients together. Both recovered and Peter never smoked a cigarette again. Cassius also had an anxious time after swallowing a needle and cotton he had taken from the sideboard. We had to wait for it to emerge.

At the end of this star-spangled season, we left Huddersfield. My days in rep were over, but I loved it better than anything I have ever done in my life

because everything changed each week. Your part, hair, voice and clothes all changed. Nowadays, actors don't get the experience of playing different roles and they therefore don't get the discipline.

From Huddersfield, Peter went to understudy, and then gain a part, at the Whitehall Theatre, in *Reluctant Heroes*, my brother Brian's first success there. His farces were to continue unabated at the Whitehall for sixteen consecutive years, beating the record created at the Aldwych Theatre in the twenties and thirties for staging more than ten consecutive years of farce.

It was pleasing to see Brian making such a success of his career, especially after I had given him that helping hand when he was seventeen and just starting out. I would join him for much of his run at the Whitehall, but before that I was more preoccupied with starting a family.

6
Happy Families

While Peter was at the Whitehall Theatre, we took a room with our old friends Margaret Jackson and Michael Peake at their house in Belsize Park, North London. It was a large house, but one room wasn't really big enough for two people and a by now large dog. I even cooked large meals on a tiny stove, which was really only a grill and a burner. I loved taking Cassius for walks on Parliament Hill fields, with the magnificent view of London, but this couldn't continue.

We decided to buy a house and, meanwhile, lived with Peter's parents. Borrowing £300 from Peter's father and £300 from mine, we found a house in nearby Golders Green, turned it into two flats and let out the top one to pay off the loan.

It had an enormous garden with an allotment at the end, from which we had every fruit you could imagine. It was like

being back at my parents' home during childhood. I don't think I bought a tin of fruit for the six years we lived there. I bottled and bottled and bottled.

I thought I would never get pregnant. We had tried for a baby ever since we had married. I longed for one so much. One day, Margaret Jackson came round and told me she was expecting a baby. I was devastated and overcome with jealousy because I had tried for a baby for so long. Indeed, it was one of my ambitions in life. I had done everything—taken my temperature, waved my legs in the air, had sex at night and travelled down to London the next morning to have the sperm tested, and had my tubes blown out at Hammersmith Hospital. That was agony and the doctor said I was making a fuss because no one else complained. I can only presume that I must have had something to blow out because the pain lasted for twenty-four hours.

After Margaret's visit, I went to bed that night and prayed, 'God, please let me have a baby, too.' The flat upstairs was let to a couple with a new baby and I thought having babies might be infectious. It was. Five weeks later, I was

pregnant, too. When Brian's wife, Elspet, heard, she decided she would have one as well. Suddenly, everyone was having a baby.

But, after three years of trying for a baby and all the problems in getting pregnant, I suffered a bit of a rough time during pregnancy. Because I was at risk of losing my baby, the doctor sent me to the septic abortion ward at Hendon Isolation Hospital. 'I don't want to lose my baby,' I said.

All the girls there had got rid of their babies, some in the most awful circumstances, even pushing needles up themselves. Some were living in one room with two children already and simply could not cope with more.

It was a dreadful ward, like a prison. We weren't even allowed screens round our beds for toilet purposes. No wonder constipation abounded! Peter's father, a retired doctor in his eighties, trudged round every day to see me. I used to look forward so much to his visits, he being a wise man who knew how to calm my troubled spirit, because it really was a month of hell.

Eventually, I was released and went back to Hornsea to have a bit of mothering.

Not that my mother was in any way demonstrative. The only time I remember her putting her arms round me was the day General Leclerc's army marched into Paris and I knew my then boyfriend Charles was there, but that was going back a few years.

However, she did make me some much needed maternity clothes and I returned to Golders Green and my greatly neglected Peter and Cassius. Peter had been preparing for my brother Brian's new Whitehall Theatre production, *Dry Rot*, which he was stage directing, and the first night was getting nearer.

That night, 30 August 1954, proved to be the hottest of the year. There I was, pregnant, and all my friends were equally pregnant. It really was very funny. Equally funny was the play, written by John Chapman. It ran to packed houses from the beginning.

One night, I woke up and discovered the waters had broken a month early. So Peter carted me off to Hampstead Maternity Hospital, where they told me the baby was on its way and to be patient. I was still being patient three days later. Then, I suddenly had tummy ache and told the

nurse I needed something for wind. She replied that she had known many a bout of wind turn into a baby.

Sure enough, at 12.15 am, on 6 December 1954, Nigel was born. Oh the joy! This was the moment I had waited for all my life, a baby of my own. Because he was early, he was jaundiced and so a bright-yellow baby used to come to me for feeds. Peter came to see him, looked at all the other babies and said, 'Ours is the best.'

There had been a bit of a mix-up over the weights, though. The woman who'd had a baby just after me had one that weighed in at ten-and-a-half pounds. I received a telegram from my father, which read, 'Congratulations on arrival of Beefeater.' I really didn't know what he meant, until I discovered the hospital had muddled the weights and mine was seven pounds. Fortunately, they couldn't muddle the babies—mine was so obviously Peter's.

We went home and Mummy came to stay for a few days, but when she had to go home I cried. 'I don't know how to look after babies,' I said. 'I do,' said Peter, flippantly. So we were all right, apparently!

Nigel was an enchanting baby, always laughing. We came down on the train from Hornsea with Elspet and her second baby, Louisa. The two babies sat on our knees and Nigel started to laugh, cackling all the way to King's Cross while Louisa coohed and aahed. He laughed at everything and everyone, and continued to do so until the time came for me to earn some much needed money.

He was fifteen months old when I went to understudy at the Whitehall Theatre, where Brian was still enjoying such great success with his stage farces. I was not away long each day and I had the most wonderful babysitters. However, they weren't Nigel's mother and he changed from being a happy little boy to a sad one. So I started taking him to the theatre with me for matinées and, by the time he was two-and-a-half, he was mimicking Brian falling over on stage and knew some of the lines.

Nigel was always one for playing with things that weren't his toys. We bought him a toy car and he played with the box for months, then gouged the headlamps out of the car to see how they worked!

Much later, we took him to the film studios at Shepperton, where they were

dismantling the sets from *The Guns of Navarone,* the Second World War epic starring Gregory Peck and David Niven, which won an Oscar for its special-effects. We took Nigel into the tunnels and he loved that. We also saw piles of good wood being taken apart and asked if we could have a plank. They let us take one, we bought string, nails and a hammer, and Nigel played for hours on end making patterns with the string. I think it was the best present he'd ever had.

Before that, when Nigel was three, I had to go into hospital for a major operation. I had to have a myomectomy, which meant having fibroid tumours removed from my uterus. Everything went wrong and, instead of being there for ten days, I was in for a month. Nigel started to sleepwalk and the ward sister said he must have been looking for me and therefore should come to the hospital to see me. I shall never forget the joy on Nigel's face when he did—it was wonderful. After that, he was all right and didn't sleepwalk any more.

I had been feeling very ill in hospital and the staff doctors told me I was a hypochondriac. The sister, who had been

off duty that weekend, returned to see me staggering across the ward. She clapped her hands and everything started to happen. I had heat treatment, blood transfusions, a visit from a specialist and short-wave treatment, where they used pads on the inflammation. You name it, I had it! The sister was a great nurse and knew exactly what to do, and we became great friends. Although she has since emigrated to New Zealand, we still write to one another and even meet when she comes over for a visit.

The night I had a blood transfusion, after internal haemorrhaging, wasn't very pleasant and there were seven people in my room at once, trying to make me laugh. Godfrey Harrison, who wrote the radio comedy series *Life of Bliss* and was a very funny man, was one of those there firing the jokes. But that was the last thing I wanted and I wished them all a million miles away. The following day, the specialist said to me, 'Not so many visitors.' I told him that I didn't want any. I hated visitors in hospital.

After coming out of hospital, I spent a long time convalescing. Peter and I took a bungalow on the Sussex coast, at

By the time younger brother Brian *(second left)*
was born, there were four Rix children – Sheila *(right)*
also having a sister, Nora and a brother, Malcolm.

Sheila's first vivid memory is of being
a bridesmaid at cousin Walter's wedding *(left)*
and leaving a puddle in the aisle.

Sheila *(centre)* showed her acting potential
at the age of eleven in a school production
of *The Windmill Man.*

She also played leading roles in her mother's
Passion Plays during her teens.

On leaving Stratford-upon-Avon College of Drama in the summer of 1939 *(above left)*, Sheila had little time for acting with the outbreak of war and *(right)* joined the WAAF.

Sheila had plenty of rep experience behind her when Basil Radford *(right)* joined brother Brian's company (including Peter Mercier, second right) for *Blind Goddess* at Bridlington in 1949.

Sheila met Peter Mercier in rep and enjoyed more than forty happy years with him.

Sheila and Peter married on Easter Monday 1951, with no time for a honeymoon because he was in the middle of a stage tour.

Ralph Lynn *(left)*, famous as the great *farceur* of the twenties and thirties at the Aldwych Theatre, joined the company at Huddersfield for a new play – and couldn't remember his lines.

Lady Bracknell, in *The Importance of Being Earnest* at Margate, was a role that brought with it a script of wonderful wit, courtesy of Oscar Wilde, and a sumptuous costume.

Giving birth
to Nigel
gave Sheila
and Peter
the child
they craved.

The family with two of their many dogs,
Cassius and Co-Co.

Good friend Peter Butterworth gets a panful of spaghetti from Nicholas Parsons as Sheila looks on in *Uproar in the House*, one of her many Whitehall Theatre farces.

Baby Michael *(left)*, became Sheila's second grandchild, joining brother David, pictured with Sheila's son Nigel and daughter-in-law Rosina.

In 1972 Sheila acquired a new 'family' when she joined *Emmerdale Farm*. Left to right: Frederick Pyne, Jo Kendall, Andrew Burt, Toke Townley, Sheila and Frazer Hines.

Sheila was joined by brother Brian on the *Emmerdale* set in 1973 when he dropped in for a look round the farmhouse.

Cassius No 2 was another of Sheila's many
beloved dogs, here staying in Leeds while recording
of *Emmerdale* took place.

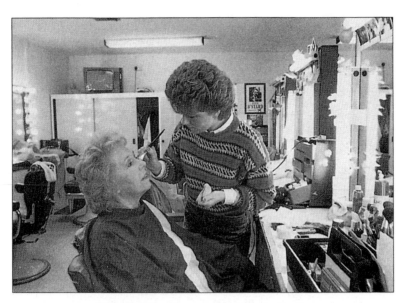

Sheila in the make-up chair
before filming an episode of *Emmerdale*.

In the studio
for the filming of *Emmerdale*.

Beckindale celebrates
with a Queen's Silver Jubilee party.

Emmerdale's tenth anniversary was a time for
celebration. Back row, left to right: Ronald Magill,
Arthur Pentelow, Clive Hornby; middle:
Frederick Pyne, Jean Rogers, Sheila, Helen Weir;
front: Toke Townley.

One of the last pictures of husband Peter,
this was taken on a holiday in France shortly
before his death in 1993.

Only a short time later, Sheila was called
upon to take Annie through a screen wedding
with actor Bernard Archard . . .

As Annie, Sheila has presided over
countless rows between sons Jack and Joe
(Clive Hornby and Frazer Hines).

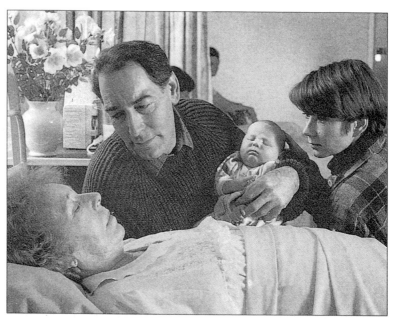

Sarah and Jack take baby Victoria
to see Annie in hospital.

With Jean Rogers and the Emmerdale Rose
at the Chelsea Flower Show.

Eamonn Andrews
nabs Sheila for *This is Your Life*.

Carol singing
at Christmas in Beckindale.

Angmering-on-Sea, where I now live. We were there for a month and the sun never came out. It rained, blew and even washed a dead cow up on the beach—and we had a right time getting the stinking thing away. Then, in September of that year, Peter's mother rented the bungalow for three weeks and the sun never disappeared. Good old sod's law! I'm a Jonah with holidays. When the sun sees me packing a case, in it goes.

We moved to Ashtead, in Surrey, when Nigel was small. He had no friends in Golders Green and they were not the sort of people with whom we wanted him to play. Our new house was huge, with five bedrooms, a hall as big as a sitting-room and two vast living-rooms.

A few days before moving there, we had a minor car crash. A drunk rushed out on to a pedestrian crossing, Peter had to brake sharply, the car behind crashed into us and I suffered whiplash. The result of that and packing for the move gave me a bad back, from which I have never recovered.

At Ashtead, we made the mistake of sending Nigel to a new school in the middle of term, so we took him away to a private school in Epsom after two terms.

He was a clever little boy but would know all the answers without knowing how to reach them, and the school was troubled. We took him to a child psychiatrist, who said that standard education would not do him any favours and he should go to a school where the education was different. This was a blow to us because it meant moving away from our beautiful house.

We managed to get Nigel into the school recommended by the psychiatrist, Michael Hall in Forest Row, East Sussex, and he loved it. They wanted him to go as a boarder, but we couldn't bear to live without him, so we decided to move again—after only three years in Ashtead. We were not able to move immediately, so Peter's mother took Nigel to school and stayed at a guest-house.

During that time, I had my third miscarriage in two years and was devastated. I longed for a companion for Nigel, and Peter was hoping for a baby girl, but it was not to be. We kept trying, but I simply did not get pregnant again. I was one of four children and wanted four myself. Having babies was one of my ambitions in life, but I have given birth to two and can at least be thankful for that.

It soon became my turn to live in a hotel, the Ashdown Forest, situated on a golf course close to where A. A. Milne wrote *Winnie-the-Pooh*. We used to take Cassius for walks on the golf course opposite and he never failed to come home with at least three golf balls.

Finally, we found a house at Chelwood Gate, five miles from the school, with an acre of land, mostly laid to grass. We made many friends there, including the late Peter Butterworth, star of Carry On films and children's television programmes. He was one of the funniest men to have at a party, as was his wife, comedienne Janet Brown, who is tee-total. She would drink Coca-Cola and get as high and happy on that as we would on alcohol.

Peter had taken up acting in a prisoner-of-war camp after being shot down by the Germans while serving in the Fleet Air Arm during the Second World War. He took part in a concert party—apparently for the sole purpose of making a din while other prisoners were trying to escape—and caught the acting bug. Unfortunately, the fifty officers who got out were recaptured and shot.

It was during a summer show in

Scarborough that Peter met Janet Brown and they later married. In recent years, while I have been working on *Emmerdale*, their son Tyler has been at the Yorkshire Television studios in the comedy series *Home to Roost* and playing the Reverend Candy in *The Darling Buds of May.*

By the time we had moved to Chelwood Gate, I had given up acting at the Whitehall Theatre after deciding that Nigel needed mothering, not smothering. We were also thinking about adopting a child, so I wrote to the Sailors' Orphan Home in Hull, where my mother was on the committee, spending her time endlessly raising money. So Nora Dora Applecora—as we called her—came into our lives. We rechristened her Linda and, after the first ten days, we said we'd like to adopt her. Our solicitor, an adopted child himself, suggested 'Wait!' How wise he was.

At first, the girl was all charm, even at four years old, and could twist the men around her little finger. However, one day, Peter was in London making a television programme and Linda was left with me. She screamed, cried, had tantrums, wet her bed, defecated in the bath and quarrelled with Nigel.

Poor Nigel had been told to share his toys with Linda. One day, he was playing with his cards and was told to give some to Linda. He didn't want to because they were special, so Peter said, 'Give her some or she gets the lot.' Nigel refused and the cards were given to her. She turned to me and, in what I can only describe as an evil voice, said, 'You see, I've got the lot,' and stuck her tongue out.

Things went from bad to worse, so I wrote to the home and asked them to take her back, which they did. I think she was happier there anyway, because they had recreation grounds, a swimming pool and her friends, about whom she talked incessantly.

So ended a period of ten weeks that I would not like to repeat. Our au pair, Marie France, took Linda to London with her new doll's pram, toys and clothes, and handed her over. When Marie came back, she said how wonderful it was not to have to listen to perpetual screaming. Linda had already been sent for adoption once before she came to us and was returned twice afterwards. She had such personality and I'm sure is a lovely woman now, but life in an orphanage obviously suited her

better than with a family. So ended that chapter.

But no sooner had our life settled down to normal than Peter began to feel unhappy at the Whitehall Theatre and could hardly bear to go on stage at night. He simply lost his nerve and never acted again. At that time, he had been having pills for his nerves for quite a while and, suddenly, he just couldn't take it any longer.

So, when *One for the Pot* finished, we decided that he would stay at home with Nigel and I would work at the Whitehall again. It was quite a long way—twenty minutes to the railway station, fifty minutes on the train to London, then a bus ride to Trafalgar Square—so I'm not surprised Peter cracked up a bit, especially with doing television programmes as well.

When Peter decided he wanted to run a pub, it was my turn to leave the theatre. He heard that the tenancy of the Anchor Inn at Hartfield, just a short distance away, was up for grabs, went for an interview and got it. Peter always had great charm, but I wish he hadn't been so successful this time.

We sold our house, threw away all the dilapidated pub carpets, eiderdowns and

other things on which we had spent a fortune, then bought everything new. It was a seventeenth-century building with low doorways and Nigel had a quaint room that he loved. However, I bumped my head every time I went in, no matter how much I tried to remember. I would fall flat on my back.

In the middle of winter, there was thick snow and we had a burst pipe in the kitchen, producing six inches of water. Max, our Alsatian, was floating around in his basket.

I settled down to running a pub, polishing floors, making up fires, chopping wood, making sandwiches, cooking for people I didn't even like and helping behind the bar as rarely as possible. Our so-called friends would arrive at closing time and, of course, stayed and we would end up footing the bill. That's how we lost so much money.

The night after I finally left the Whitehall, Peter said to me in bed, 'This life is not for us.' I couldn't have agreed more. There were fun nights—usually Fridays, when a jolly crowd came in—but mostly it was the same people with the same stories day after day.

It was really a summer pub, but we had it in winter. When the brewery suggested we stay through the summer and get our money back, we told them we would rather have our health and strength. We lost about £2,000, which was a lot of money then, but we didn't care.

Peter and I found a nice unfurnished house to rent in Tonbridge and went to Spain with Nigel for a well earned holiday. I returned to the theatre and found it too far to travel from home, so we bought a house in Hinchley Wood with three bedrooms—one of them very big—and a large kitchen, as well as woods for the dogs directly opposite. Perfect.

The only drawback was you had to walk through the sitting-room from the kitchen to go upstairs, which was like having a perpetual corridor. We eventually solved that by adding a corridor and dining-room downstairs, and another loo and upstairs playroom/study for Nigel. The builders told us it would take six weeks, but they were there six months.

Nigel left Michael Hall and went to Ewell Castle, an all-boys' school, and Peter went to work for Donald Albery as relief front-of-house manager at his four theatres,

the New Theatre (which was later renamed the Albery), Wyndham's, the Criterion and the Piccadilly. We were all back in business and, to cap it all, I passed my driving test at the first attempt. It was the long winter of 1963 and doing a three-point turn was a work of art with snow piled high at both sides of the roads. I was no longer the helpless little wife who needed driving everywhere. I even went on tour to every major city in the country.

While doing a summer season in Morecambe, I shared a house with Helen Jessop, who had been leading lady in my brother Brian's first Whitehall hit, *Reluctant Heroes,* and subsequently starred in other farces of his such as *Chase Me, Comrade!* and *Stand By Your Bedouin.*

By the time I had finished a meal, she had taken only two mouthfuls, having been brought up in India, where to talk over a meal came before eating it. Nigel came to stay and made friends with Julie Kershaw, daughter of the house's owner, who lived just round the comer. Nigel and Julie were inseparable. There was a swimming pool in the garden and the two were forever splashing around in it.

After the season in Morecambe, Nigel

changed schools again and went to a state one, where he was very happy, particularly because it was mixed. It was there that he met and wooed Rosina, the girl he was eventually to marry. By then, my career had taken two turns.

7
What a Farce!

Many actors deride farce because they don't know how to do it. In fact, it's the most difficult form of acting, completely different from comedy and drama. The key to it is timing and knowing when to stop a laugh. It's also important not to send it up—that's where many people go wrong. They think they just have to pull funny faces, put on a funny voice and clothes, and people will laugh, but you must have a good story.

The English farces that my brother Brian began staging in the fifties were different from their French predecessors. Modern farce began in seventeenth-century France with Molière and was followed there by Labiche and Feydeau. The Gallic variety has always been filled to the brim with sex, but English farce developed altogether differently, writers such as Ben Travers and Vernon Sylvaine relying on buffoonery and double-meanings to get laughs. When

trousers were dropped it was more a sign of loss of dignity than anything sexual.

My chance to act in farce came when Wynne Clark left the cast of Brian's Whitehall Theatre production of *Dry Rot* to perform Shakespeare at the Old Vic and her understudy, Beryl Ede, took over. I stood in for her, understudying the part of the awful policewoman Sergeant Fire, and was also understudy for Cecily Paget-Bowman, as the Colonel's Lady.

Dry Rot, the story of three bookies trying to fix a horse race, was Brian's second farce at the Whitehall, following *Reluctant Heroes*, which ran for four years. It could probably have gone on for much longer, but Brian decided enough was enough. The writer of the new one, John Chapman, had been Brian's understudy in the first show and has become one of Britain's top playwrights in the genre.

As well as my brother, *Dry Rot* starred John Slater, Basil Lord and Larry Noble. By the time I joined the production, in 1956, the original cast had made a film version, with my husband assisting the director, Maurice Elvey. Also in the film was Ronald Shiner, who had become a screen star following his success in *Worm's*

Eye View, based on a stage farce he had appeared in about workshy RAF 'erks' billeted on a suburban family. He first worked with Brian on the big screen version of *Reluctant Heroes*—described by one critic as 'a sort of earlier version of *Carry On Sergeant*'—which had been my brother's first venture into the world of cinema.

In fact, the banjo-playing music-hall and film star George Formby had been offered Brian's role in *Reluctant Heroes* but, when he went to see a Friday matinée of the play, Brian was ill and unable to go on stage that afternoon. The resulting performance was so poorly received that George turned down the part, which meant Brian was able to repeat his Whitehall role in the film.

The film of *Dry Rot* had Ronald Shiner cast in John Slater's role as the cockney bookmaker, Alf Tubbe, and Sid James took over the part of Flash Harry, played by Basil Lord on stage. Sid, who was born in South Africa, was already making his name as Tony Hancock's partner on radio and television, and went on to appear in many of the Carry On films, as well as several situation comedies on TV, most

memorably *George and the Dragon* and *Bless This House.*

Peggy Mount, who had just made her name as the fearsome Mrs Hornett in the stage and screen versions of *Sailor Beware!* and went on to become the star of television comedies such as *The Larkins* and *George and the Dragon* (with Sid), was brought in as a star name. So was Joan Sims, at that time known for her film appearances in *Doctor in the House* and *The Belles of St Trinian's,* and later to become a regular with the Carry On team. Brian, of course, recreated his role as bookie's runner Fred Phipps.

Releasing the film while the stage play was still playing to packed houses did Brian and the Whitehall team no harm at all. When I joined the *Dry Rot* cast there, Leo Franklyn had taken over the role played by John Slater, who had left to take the production on tour.

Leo, who was a very serious man but also very funny, went on to appear in another seven of Brian's farces over a period of seventeen years and was one of a whole group of people with whom I became great friends. He was also the father of William Franklyn, who had acted

in repertory theatre with me in Margate. William, who had spent ten years in Australia as a child while his father was working there, travelling around in an old Pullman car, was also one of Brian's cricketing pals.

My Whitehall début came when, one night, Cecily Paget-Bowman was taken ill and I was told to stand by in the wings to take over as the Colonel's Lady. Halfway through one scene, when she was acting with the Colonel, Cecily felt faint and staggered off stage. I went straight on and picked up the next line as though nothing had happened. There was a murmur from the audience, but I just carried on with the scene and they accepted me as if I had been there all the time. I had never previously understudied, so this had not happened to me before, but it was good experience. I wasn't frightened suddenly having to stand in for someone because I had heard the play night after night and knew all the lines.

At that time, Peter was stage directing the production and eventually took over a role played by John Chapman, the writer. I didn't really feel I was going back to acting at that time, just understudying. We had

understudy rehearsals and I used to go into the audience to watch the show so that I was clued up about what was going on.

I didn't have to be on stage until half an hour before the curtain went up and left when the principal actors made their last entrance, so I wasn't away from home too long. However, I often felt guilty about going to work, leaving a fifteen-month-old baby at home, but we needed the money. In the house, we had just a cooker, a fridge, a chair, a double bed and a single bed that we used as a sofa. That was the extent of our furniture. With my first Whitehall pay packets, we bought two armchairs from Selfridges.

However, one unhappy memory of working at the theatre was walking home from Brent station one night after a performance and hearing someone walking on the opposite side of the road. He seemed to be trying to catch me up, then I felt a hand round my throat, at which I screamed—not a high-pitched scream, but a low, contralto one. My assailant was obviously frightened and ran off up the road.

I pressed the doorbells of houses in the road so that I could phone the police,

but no one answered—their television sets must have been on too loud. Not until I arrived home could I get to the telephone and then, of course, the man was miles away. By the time the police came round, I was over the shock because I'm one of those stupid people who always laughs at adversity. Seeing me laughing, the police probably thought I was having them on.

One of the perks of Peter's job as a stage director was bringing home 'props' that were used in the play, such as sausages and bottles of Guinness. When we decided Guinness wasn't really to our taste, Peter changed a line in the play and ended up bringing back bottles of Mackesons, which we both enjoyed!

After Peter worked on the film of *Dry Rot*, we were able to afford a car—a new Ford Popular, costing £200. It was wonderful because, for the first time since we had our Austin Seven, we could get around without walking.

Dry Rot came to an end in 1958 after a four-year run and we immediately started work on the next farce, *Simple Spymen*. It ran for more than three years and, again, I was understudy, this time to Joan Sanderson, who went on to play rather

domineering women on television, such as Miss Ewell in *Please Sir!* and Prunella Scales's mother in *After Henry*. She was also superb as the custodian of Chequers in *Anyone for Denis?*, the satirical comedy about Margaret and Denis Thatcher, on both stage and television.

Before opening in London with *Simple Spymen*, we went on a four-week tour and, when we performed in Hull, we stayed with Mummy. From there, we had to go to Stoke-on-Trent, which proved too much for our Ford Popular. It didn't have any heating and the windscreen wipers suddenly packed up. We had to keep stopping to clear the screen and Peter's feet became so cold and wet that he could hardly drive.

Following the horrendous journey, we found our digs to be terrible. There were three tiny pieces of coal burning in the fireplace, and there was no fire at all in the bedroom that Nigel shared with Peter's mother, who had come to look after him. The next morning, we gave the landlady extra money and asked her to buy coal because we had to have heat. She didn't even have hot water for a bath. Somehow, we got through that week, but

it was really awful. Some of the digs at which actors had to stay were horrendous. At least Nigel enjoyed looking round the potteries in Stoke and was especially taken with the man whose job it was to break the ones that were not perfect.

Next, we arrived in Birmingham with nowhere to stay after a message that our landlady had been taken ill. In the end, we stayed at a hotel, sent Peter's mother home—because we couldn't afford to have her there as well—and took Nigel to the theatre every evening. He began to get tired and fractious, so the producer told me not to come in and they would send for me if I was needed. I didn't go to work at all that week.

Finally we opened at the Whitehall Theatre and enjoyed another great success. After a row with Brian, Joan Sanderson —who had such a lovely personality—left the production and I took over as Mrs Byng. I was supposed to be playing the part for two weeks, until someone else was found, but they were so pleased with me that I was kept on as the leading lady. Peter actually taught Joan Sanderson to drive, as he did Andrew Sachs, who was in the play and had previously appeared

on stage with me at Bexhill Rep.

As Mrs Byng, I got a laugh before I had even opened my mouth. My first appearance was in the second act, sitting down doing needlework. I had to get up and press the bell to summon the waiter, then sit down on the needle, which created an immediate laugh. It was a very funny part, and there aren't many for women in farce, although John Chapman and Ray Cooney's plays proved to have more than the old Aldwych farces.

During the run of *Simple Spymen*, Mummy, Daddy, Brian, Elspet and Louisa went to Climping, in West Sussex, for a holiday. Daddy wanted me to go as well, so Brian gave me a week off. Nigel and I set off on the tube, which stopped at Camden Town and couldn't go any further, so we hailed a taxi. On the journey to Victoria Station, the driver braked suddenly to let someone over a crossing and I smashed my face against the window. I ended up going to hospital with a bloody nose, black eyes and whiplash.

I wasn't fit to go to Climping, so returned home. However, I went a couple of days later and we all had a wonderful holiday. It was a good place to take

children, with a babysitting service, so you could leave your children and enjoy dinner in peace.

Ever since the experience in the taxi, I've had a bad back and neck, and have been going to a chiropractor. I tried traction and other treatments, but they only made it worse, so I decided alternative medicine was right for me. I received £16 in compensation, but the episode must have cost me thousands of pounds in pain and inconvenience. Later we had the accident where a drunk ran across a zebra crossing and I suffered whiplash again.

During this time at the Whitehall, the company was also doing farces for BBC television on Sunday evenings. So Brian was not only staging enormously popular theatre productions, but also putting the hit shows and others specially made for television on the small screen. We couldn't just do the ones we were performing at the Whitehall—and, later, the Garrick—because they were so successful and long-running that, in all of Brian's twenty-seven years in London's West End, he staged only eleven plays.

He had started his association with the BBC by doing excerpts from *Reluctant*

Heroes in 1952 and, four years later, was asked to put on regular shows. This he did for seventeen years, in one-offs, a series called *Dial Rix*, and then *Six of Rix*. They were the only programmes to give *Sunday Night at the London Palladium*, over on ITV, a run for its money.

For the television productions, we performed the shows at the Whitehall Theatre in front of an audience, except for one, which was made at the BBC's Shepherd's Bush studios. It was extra money and made me feel I was doing something worthwhile. We always felt more at home performing in the natural setting of the Whitehall Theatre. Joan Sims was one of those who joined the regulars for TV productions.

I shall never forget the first one I did. As I was about to make my entrance, Brian said, 'Don't forget, Sheila, the eyes of Hornsea are on you.' My legs turned to jelly. Television programmes were all made live in those days, so everyone was much more tense anyway, whereas today you can always record something again—although you feel awful about it when it happens.

One show we did for the BBC, in 1960, was *Boobs in the Wood*, a farce

and pantomime all rolled into one, written by Ray Cooney and Tony Hilton, and choreographed by Duggie Squires. Carole Shelley, who later found fame in *The Odd Couple* on Broadway and in the film, was brought in as Principal Boy after Maggie Smith had been approached but was unavailable. I played the nursemaid and Peter was a wicked baron.

At the dress rehearsal, we had an audience and they laughed themselves hoarse. The bell fell on Brian's head when it was supposed to and everything went like clockwork. I don't know what happened on the night of the actual performance, but it was a disaster, with hardly any laughs and the most awful reviews. Brian had just signed a new, three year contract with the BBC and this was hardly the best start.

The sad thing is that it could have been revived and performed in a theatre, but the script and tapes were lost by the BBC. It's one of the funniest scripts I've seen in my life. Also, the production was accompanied by a real-life episode that could have been the basis of a script for a farce, with Brian's wife, Elspet, going into labour during rehearsals and giving birth to their second son Jonathan.

As well as television, Brian had, of course, branched out into films. After *Reluctant Heroes* and *Dry Rot* had been adapted for the cinema, I appeared in two of his pictures, *The Night We Dropped a Clanger*, in 1959, and *The Night We Got the Bird*, a year later.

The first, a wartime comedy, was written specially by John Chapman, with Whitehall regulars such as Leo Franklyn, Larry Noble and John Chapman joined by Cecil Parker—a stalwart of about seventy films up to that time, excelling in comedy roles such as in *The Ladykillers*—playing an absent-minded Air Vice-Marshal called Buk-passer.

There were also three stars from the Carry On team, William Hartnell (who played Sergeant Grimshaw in *Carry On Sergeant*, Sergeant Major Bullimore in the television situation comedy *The Army Game* and, later, the original Doctor Who), Hattie Jacques (the matronly star who also appeared on radio as Sophie Tuckshop in *ITMA* and Agatha Danglebody in *Educating Archie*, as well as with Tony Hancock in his original radio shows, and later on television as Eric Sykes's sister in the long-running *Sykes* series) and Leslie

Phillips (who has acted in film comedies such as *Crooks Anonymous, The Fast Lady* and the Doctor films, before reviving his career with more serious roles on television in recent years).

It was quite daunting turning up at a film studio for the first time. In the canteen, we met big stars from the other pictures being made there, and really we were small fry compared with many of them. The most frustrating part of making a film was having to sit in your dressing-room for hours on end before being called, and then producing the small amount required.

During filming, which took place at Shepperton Studios, I shared a dressing-room with Liz Fraser, another film star who was drafted in to supplement the Whitehall team. The first time I walked in, she wasn't there, but I found a couple of azaleas in the bath that she was soaking—with the intention of getting them to come back to life. I thought they were drowning, so naturally let the water out. She was livid! I should say, though, that Liz is a good-hearted person who has done much charity work over the years.

One person I got on with particularly

well was Jimmy Komisarjevsky, who was the first assistant director. His father, Theodore, a Venice-born Russian director and designer who became a naturalised Briton, had put on some wonderful productions at Stratford-upon-Avon while I was there. I saw two of them, *The Comedy of Errors* and *Twelfth Night*, which both showed him to have a flair for the unusual. He had previously directed Randle Ayrton in *King Lear* at Stratford and Donald Wolfit in *Antony and Cleopatra* at the New Theatre, London, and was also renowned for his productions of Russian plays in this country.

As a WAAF girl who seemed to spend all her time giggling in corners and doing silly things, I didn't have much to do in *The Night We Dropped a Clanger*, appearing in only about four scenes. It was a very funny film and Brian played two parts, a heroic Air Force officer sent to France on a secret mission, and his double—an oafish lavatory attendant—sent to Cairo to confuse the Nazis. Of course, it all goes wrong and the two end up on each other's plane and, thus, in the wrong place. The story was a bit of a spoof of *I Was Monty's Double*, the tale of an actor being

154

hired to pose as General Montgomery in Africa in a bid to fool the Germans. Cecil Parker had appeared in that, too, only the previous year.

Brian, unfortunately, not only had to contend with playing two characters— sometimes both seen on the screen at the same time, thanks to a process called 'travelling matte'—but was also suffering from boils all over his body, so he had to sit down with great care, aided by an air ring. We were also performing *Simple Spymen* at the Whitehall in the evenings. Brian could have done without such a busy workload at that time. The boils lasted for a full eighteen months, but they have never returned, thankfully.

The Night We Dropped a Clanger was one of six films that Rank had commissioned Sydney Box to make for its national circuit and was probably the only one to make money. Sydney had produced war-time propaganda films before setting up his own company. He offered Brian a contract to make three pictures, but that lapsed after Sydney fell ill. Brian then switched to British Lion to make my next film with him, *The Night We Got the Bird*, again directed by Darcy

155

Conyers—a former actor who had moved behind the camera—but produced by Rix-Conyers Films, the company he had set up with Brian.

Adapted by Ray Cooney, Tony Hilton and Darcy Conyers from Basil Thomas's play *The Love Birds,* which starred Ronald Shiner, *The Night We Got the Bird* featured Ronald recreating his stage role as a dead man returning in the guise of a South American parrot, haunting his widow and her new husband. Brian and Dora Bryan—who had also been in the original stage production—played a honeymoon couple constantly interrupted while trying to find a phoney antique bed that Ronald had sold under false pretences. Dora had been seen most often on screen in comedy roles, switching between her native Lancashire accent and a cockney one.

The Whitehall regulars included Brian, Leo Franklyn, John Slater and Basil Lord. We were joined by Irene Handl (another performer celebrated for her cockney characterisations in films, and on radio with Arthur Askey and Tony Hancock, before success on television in the situation comedy *For the Love of Ada),* John Le Mesurier (later of *Dad's Army*

television fame), Robertson Hare (that old *farceur* from the Aldwych Theatre) and Terry Scott (who, as well as being in the Carry On films, had already had a successful stage and television partnership with Bill Maynard and was about to team up with Hugh Lloyd, before his long-running success with June Whitfield). Liz Fraser was in the cast for this one, too.

I had the part of a teacher in a boarding school and, again, it was a role that required a certain amount of giggling and running about chasing girls. Most of my scenes were with Wynne Clark—who played the headmistress—and the girls in the dormitory. It was Wynne, of course, who gave me my break at the Whitehall by leaving and creating room for me as an understudy. She stayed with Peter and me at our home in Ashtead while we were making the film and, every morning, a car would arrive to take us to Shepperton Studios. Unfortunately, *The Night We Got the Bird* was panned by the critics and not a great box-office success. Brian made only a few more films after that, preferring to continue with what he knew best—getting laughs on the stage—although television audiences were to see the Whitehall crowd

for many years to come.

Back on stage, *Simple Spymen* came to a close and was followed by *One for the Pot*, written by Ray Cooney and Tony Hilton. Before it reached the Whitehall, the play was called *Dickory Dock*—the leading character was called Hickory—and it was tried out at Richmond Theatre, with Ray Cooney taking one of the leading roles.

In the West End, *One for the Pot* proved to be another long-running hit, with perhaps the best first night we ever enjoyed. It continued to pull in audiences for almost three years. Winston Churchill, Prince Charles and Princess Anne were among the many VIPs who came to see us.

Following the appointment of our usual director, Wally Douglas, as programme controller of Westward Television, Henry Kendall took over the role. As an actor, he had been a major screen star of the thirties—and later appeared in Brian's 1961 film *Nothing Barred*—and he also had a long stage career. Unfortunately, Henry was an ill man and died of a heart attack during the play's run. In fact, he was on holiday in the south of France at the time and Brian and Elspet were

holidaying only a few miles away. They received a telephone call in the early hours of the morning to inform them that Henry had collapsed and was dying. They arrived shortly before he did so. Brian then had the task of helping to arrange for the body to be transported back to Britain for cremation.

Back at the Whitehall, the cast of *One for the Pot* included Basil Lord, Leo Franklyn, Terry Scott, Larry Noble, Helen Jessop—a good friend who has since emigrated to South Africa—and Peter. I played Aunt Amy, a rather silly North Country woman, and was encased in a corset at the time because of my bad back. Poor Basil had to carry me off stage by giving me a fireman's lift but, because the corset kept me rigid, he had to hold me absolutely straight instead of fallen over his shoulder. In the end, I got sick of the corsets and threw them away. I was better without them.

During 1962, while performing *One for the Pot* in the evenings, we were, by day, making the *Dial Rix* television series for the BBC. The title came out of the opening sequence of each episode, in which Brian would be seen phoning a relative, also played by him, and the story would emanate from that telephone conversation.

Darcy Conyers, who had directed the two films I appeared in with Brian, also made the first three programmes of this nine-part series. However, his cinema background made him think a bit too big and he ended up spending too much of the budget. Therefore, Wally Douglas, who had by then resigned as programme controller of Westward Television, returned to the fold to complete it.

It was also during *One for the Pot* that Brian's company, Rix Theatrical Productions, ceased to exist as a result of being part of our father's business empire, which by then was crumbling. Brian immediately set up Brian Rix Enterprises Ltd and carried on as if nothing had happened. Unfortunately, our father and his brother did not have a limited company and all their interests, from ship-owning to theatrical productions, were their own personal liability. They fell on hard times and the bank would give them no more credit. The £90,000 that Brian had made at the Whitehall was gone.

Everything seemed to be happening during this particular stage production, because I also became pregnant. In the story, Basil and Brian painted my portrait,

so I had to sit still on the sofa and I remember thinking I was going to be sick. Sadly, it came to nothing because I lost the baby and the next two. I left *One for the Pot* three times with pregnancies, then went back. It was a dreadful time. To lose a child with a miscarriage is the most awful, depressing thing, after psyching yourself up into thinking you're having a baby. It's very painful and so unproductive. It was all rather sad, and Nigel remained a lonely boy, but that's all in the past now.

Leo Franklyn, a dashing man and great to work with throughout this string of stage hits, restored some of my humour with his 'exhibition'. He was a true friend to me, and he and his wife Mary were so kind. Leo had very elastic private parts and, believe it or not, would turn them into 'sausage on a plate', 'a flying swan' and other curios.

One celebrity to turn up in the audience at the Whitehall—and to witness Leo's 'exhibition'—was expatriate Soviet ballet dancer Rudolf Nureyev. He came to see *Chase Me, Comrade!*, our next farce, about a ballet dancer defecting from Russia. It had, of course, been inspired by his experience of seeking asylum in Paris in

1961, when he was a talented young soloist with the Kirov company. I played Mrs Riddington, the commander's wife.

We put on a party after the show and I talked to him at length, pointing out that no one knew how to pronounce his name. 'Noo-noo-noo-ryef,' he replied. After all the champagne was drunk, Leo gave Nureyev a short performance and the dancer was gobsmacked.

Margot Fonteyn, the great prima ballerina who had first partnered Nureyev in the Royal Ballet production of *Giselle* at Covent Garden in 1962, was another visitor to the theatre during *Chase Me, Comrade!*, but she was spared Leo's backstage act!

When Brian took a month's holiday, Stanley Baxter—who was already delighting television audiences with his send-ups of TV programmes and Hollywood films—took over his role in *Chase Me, Comrade!*, before taking a new production of it to Australia.

The end of the production's run at the Whitehall also saw the end of Brian's sixteen-year association with that theatre. The Whitehall's owner, Louis Cooper, died in 1961 and his general manager was sent packing by his new boss, Louis's

daughter Felice, three years later. When, in 1966, Brian tried to buy the lease of the theatre, Felice thought her new husband might want to run it himself. Although it turned out that he did not, Brian had by then left and Paul Raymond—famous as the owner of the Raymond Revuebar in London—was glad to take it off her hands.

Ironically, Brian had a financial stake in *Come Spy with Me*, the show starring Danny La Rue that subsequently opened at the Whitehall. It was Danny's West End début and the production ran to packed houses for eighteen months, establishing him as a major star.

That was a difficult time for all of us, for it was the year that our father died. He had a series of small strokes and, eventually, the living room was turned into a bedroom for him and two nurses were installed. Peter and I went to see him and he did not know us.

The next morning, I woke at 6 am longing for a cup of tea, so I went downstairs to make one and took it into the room where Daddy was sleeping. Suddenly, his quiet voice said, 'I'd like one of those.' So I leapt up and made

him one in his invalid beaker and held his head up while he drank. We talked for two hours—sensible talk. He seemed so much better.

Peter and I had to leave for London and passed Brian on the way up. We got out of our cars and I told Brian he was so much better. Alas, that was the last time he spoke and he died a few days later.

After leaving the Whitehall, we did a summer season of *Chase Me, Comrade!* in Morecambe, followed by a tour, but touring is something I would never do again—it's a soul-destroying way of living. I would rather scrub floors, which I can't do because of my arthritic knees.

In 1967, we made *One for the Pot* for television, before moving a short distance from the Whitehall to the Garrick Theatre to start Brian's repertoire idea. We opened with a Ray Cooney-Tony Hilton farce called *Stand By Your Bedouin,* starring Dickie Henderson and originally titled *Bang, Bang Beirut.* After a short run it alternated each week with *Uproar in the House* (written by Anthony Marriott and Alastair Foot), before *Let Sleeping Wives Lie* (by Harold Brooke and Kay Bannerman) was also added.

The late Dickie Henderson, then a great friend of Brian, was a major star of stage and television, where he had his own situation comedy, *The Dickie Henderson Show*, with June Laverick playing his wife. As a favourite at the London Palladium, he was a master of playing to big audiences and was marvellous in *Stand By Your Bedouin*. He even got us out of a spot of bother when the revolve that was a hidey hole for Helen Jessop's character and mine wouldn't go round because a telephone wire became stuck in it. Dickie managed to get it working again, changing lines as he did so.

Unfortunately, there were also crossed lines over Brian's repertoire concept and it turned out to be a disaster. It seemed that the public first thought we were presenting three one-act plays, then believed the plays were being taken off because they were unsuccessful. Only at the National Theatre can you do something like that, apparently. *Let Sleeping Wives Lie* continued at the Garrick and another production company took over *Uproar in the House* and staged it at the Whitehall, which was like going home.

It ran for fifteen months there, with

Nicholas Parsons and then Henry McGee starring, but I was so bored. The role of Audrey Grey was a nice part, but I had to stand on stage for what seemed like hours or else sit and say nothing. I felt myself drifting off. One night when my mind was elsewhere, Nicholas Parsons actually said my lines for me. It's very difficult to concentrate when you're bored. Audiences were thin and how the show kept going I don't know. One of the things that kept *me* going was that I had so many friends in the cast, including Peter Butterworth and Joan Sims. Peter, of course, has since died, but I shall always remember him as a terribly funny man.

When *Uproar in the House* finished, I was out of a job, which was really rather nice, having worked my socks off for so many years. Peter was Ray Cooney's general manager, organising shows in seaside resorts here, as well as in Jersey and South Africa, so we didn't have to worry about money coming in. I sat back on my haunches and played the good wife to Peter.

Once, we visited Bournemouth for the opening of a season of Ray Cooney productions. Peter, Nigel and I were

staying in a good hotel and came back to change for our evening meal. Peter did not put a tie on—after all, we were by the seaside—and, when we arrived downstairs, the head waiter would not let us in. Peter pointed to the vast dining-room, in which there were two people, and asked, 'What's the problem?' Peter had plenty of ties with him but would not wear one on a point of principle.

Refused entry to the dining-room, we went back upstairs, ordered dinner for three plus wine, and had four waiters attending us on the fifth floor. All they could charge us was four shillings each, the price for room service. So they had twelve shillings and all the inconvenience.

In 1972, Brian mounted a six-week tour of Vernon Sylvaine farces under the umbrella title *Six of Rix*. They were adapted by Michael Pertwee, who had just turned Sylvaine's *Nap Hand* into the not so successful West End show *She's Done It Again* for Brian at the Garrick Theatre.

Brian secured permission from the original playwright's widow and the result was six plays, each of fifty minutes, with two presented as a double-bill each night. At the end of every two

weeks, we recorded them for television. Unfortunately, many viewers missed the series because it coincided with the power cuts that were part of the industrial crisis that eventually brought down Edward Heath's Conservative government.

I've lost count of how many farces I've done for the BBC, but it was always nice to get the extra money. I completed the tour, earned an extra £600 from the television productions and promptly spent it on redecorating the house. So ended my long career with the Whitehall farces and with Brian.

The next time Peter and I went to Bournemouth, we stayed at Sandbanks Hotel, which in those days was paradise for children. It was there that I received my summons to Yorkshire Television for an interview that was to change my life—and take me back to the county of my childhood.

8
Emmerdale Farm

The first call to see casting director Muriel Cole came from Yorkshire Television's studios in London while I was at home. I was about to leave for the appointment when the phone rang to say she couldn't see me that day, so I thought, 'Sod Muriel Cole, whoever she is!' However, when I was in Bournemouth with Peter, another call came for me to see her, but I couldn't go. Eventually, the appointment was made and up to London I went. I found her absolutely delightful and we got on wonderfully well. Suddenly, she said, 'Come tomorrow. I might have something for you.'

So, the following day, up I trotted to London again for a meeting with producer David Goddard, casting director Sue Whatmough, director Tristan de Vere Cole and writer Kevin Laffan. I was there quite a long time and all of them were very easy to talk to. They said the new

programme for which they were casting, *Emmerdale Farm,* was scheduled to run for thirteen weeks and twenty-six episodes, but asked if I would be willing to stay for two years if it proved a success. I said I'd have to talk it over with Peter.

I went home to Esher, in Surrey, for a family conference. Nigel was busy studying for his A-levels and Peter was not well. He was also unhappy working for Ray Cooney, who we always said had the energy for two because he could do so many things at once and expected his staff to do the same. Ray was a twin and the other had died, which might explain his double-energy.

So I had all this to worry about. Thirteen weeks was nothing, but two years was something else. I phoned all my friends again and it was Linda Cooney, Ray's wife, who persuaded me to take the job. 'Don't think of two years,' she said. 'Think thirteen weeks at a time.'

The part was Annie Sugden and the story had her facing life on a Yorkshire Dales farm after the death of her husband, Jacob. The programme was based around this matriarchal figure and her two bickering sons, Jack and Joe. Jack had left home, but returned on his father's death to claim

his inheritance. This riled the younger son, Joe, who had stayed and worked on the ailing farm, whose downward spiral was largely a result of his father's drinking and neglect. The story was good and I would be at the centre of it.

So, on 26 June 1972—just five weeks after being interviewed for the part—I found myself in the reception at Yorkshire Television's Leeds studios. I was the first member of the cast to arrive and was feeling a bit motor-shocked, having driven there, so retired to the pub across the road for a large brandy—or two. Gradually, all the cast arrived and we went to The Jumbo, a famous Chinese restaurant in the city. We all got on like a house on fire and this turned out to be my second family. Afterwards, we went to a disco and David Beresford, our first unit manager on the programme, had a dance with me and said, 'I'm going to love you and love you and care for you like no one has before.' And he did.

The following morning, we had a read-through of the first few episodes. Freddie Pyne, who played farmer Matt Skilbeck, Annie's son-in-law, had arrived by then, having missed the party. I read as I always

read—to the gods. I had done dozens of television productions, but they had almost all been from the Whitehall Theatre. I couldn't understand why everyone seemed to be mumbling, but I soon found out.

Tristan, the director, taught me so much. 'Half that, half that! Down again,' he would say, until I was doing the script the right way for television. I shall always be grateful to him. Gordon Flemyng was the same when he directed. If I did something ugly or badly, he would play it back on the studio floor so that I could see what I had done wrong—a genius of an idea.

My first outdoor filming took place at Arncliffe Church for the funeral of Annie's husband, Jacob, which provided a sombre start to the serial. The church there is very old and very beautiful, with plaques lining the walls, listing all those who had taken part in a twelfth-century battle long before guns had been invented. Someone had carried a pike, someone a shield and someone had a horse, the plaques recorded. Frazer Hines, playing my younger son Joe, was in the funeral car and we soon found out that you couldn't spend long in his company without bursting into laughter. We went up that hill so many times, to

get the scene just right, that picnickers must have been amazed to see this funeral cortège going by again and again creased up with laughter. Of course, when we passed the cameras, we were very sombre.

Then came the burial in the churchyard, which was so beautiful that I flung my arms wide and proclaimed, 'Here all the summer of my life I'll stay,' which is a good quote from a play called *Duet for Two Hands*, written by John Mills's wife, Mary Hayley Bell. On the black side, the midges found a vein in my leg and I was bitten to pieces. Now, I never travel without Waspeze, which covers all sorts of bites.

For that first episode, I put into use the ivory prayer book that I had carried as a bridesmaid for my elder brother Malcolm's wedding at the start of the war. My sister, Nora, and I had those instead of bouquets and I have always used it in the programme when the occasion has arisen.

That first location filming also led to high-spirited fun at the Falcon Inn in Arncliffe, where we stayed overnight. We had all wined and dined well and, when we went to our rooms, there were applepie

beds, people were tipped out of bed and I sat up imperiously in my four-poster and shouted, 'What's going on here?' It was like being back in a school dormitory. In the end, we all settled down to sleep, but there were some thick heads next morning and I had to apologise to the landlady, who had been tight-lipped throughout the frolics, despite all the noise. Toke Townley, who played my father, Sam Pearson, had not joined in with the high spirits. He was happiest in his own solitude and when he was acting, in his own 'circle of light' as he called it.

Those first twenty-six episodes were sheer magic—poetry to me. I dashed home down the MI whenever I had a couple of days to spare, then it was up at the crack of dawn on Sunday morning. It was exhausting and I couldn't manage even one journey down the motorway these days.

At first, I stayed at Novello House, a famous theatrical digs run by Basil Hartley, who was rather dictatorial and the type to call a spade a spade, telling people outright if he did not want them to stay there.

There were other actors there from the Grand Theatre and Leeds Playhouse (now the West Yorkshire Playhouse), but they

came and went. I was the only one from *Emmerdale Farm* and began to feel very lonely when not working. So, after twelve weeks I moved to Brentwood Court, where Jo Kendall—who played Annie's daughter Peggy—Frazer Hines and director David Green, soon to join us, all lived. I was surrounded by friends and even had some of the cast to stay with me.

Every weekend, I drove south to my family, stocked up the fridge and larder, left Peter and Nigel enough to eat for a week and did all the washing and ironing. I was so bedazzled by my work that I failed to see how ill Peter was. I've never disclosed this publicly before, but he had a nervous breakdown and it was a dreadful period to go through, for all of us.

He had been showing signs of stress for some time and I took him to our former doctor, who knew him well. He recognised the fact that Peter needed help and sent him to a Harley Street doctor, who said that Peter must go into hospital for treatment. So I took him to a nursing home in Harrow-on-the-Hill, where he was given ECT. I hated this and said he should not have it, but our doctor friend argued that Peter was very ill and

175

therefore needed it.

After the ECT, he was allowed to come home for a night. I fetched him home but could not cope, he was in such a state. I phoned the nursing home and they told me to take Peter straight back. He received another dose of ECT, after which he was much better, although not 'best'. I had him at home for a few days, then took him up to Leeds, where he slowly started to mend. After a while, he went back to work, but it was too soon and, a few months later, Peter left Ray Cooney with regret and joined me in Leeds again.

In the meantime, I was being driven mad in my flat by four Turks, who lived below and seemed to laugh all night, and Frazer, who lived above and was a great one for entertaining and playing cards with his noisy friends into the small hours. I spent all my time banging on the floor or phoning Frazer to tell him to shut up. I was working hard and needed my sleep.

Another little problem arose. I was getting phone calls at 5.30 am to say, 'Shall I come up and **** you now?' Well, I didn't care what they said—they are only words—but I did object to being awoken

at that time every morning. I contacted the police and all my calls were monitored, which resulted in it ceasing, until I received a call with the same words. I thought, 'Oh, Lord! They're starting in the evening now.' This time, it turned out to be George Little, the Reverend Edward Ruskin in *Emmerdale Farm,* who officiated at the programme's first wedding, that of Janie Harker and Frank Blakey, the village blacksmith. He had heard the story and used it to put me in a flap, although he was, in fact, getting in touch to say that he was returning to the programme for a few months. He could have found a kinder way of telling me!

I couldn't sleep in that flat, so when Peter came up the first time we found one at the top of an old house, but it proved to be a mistake. Not only was it too far up for my arthritic knee, but the neighbours below—a doctor, his wife and baby—didn't have a telephone and I gave them a key so that in a dire emergency they could use ours. One night when I was on my own, I woke up to find the doctor in my room, drunk, wanting to order a taxi for his friend but unable to get one. 'Get me a taxi or I'll kill you,' he kept repeating. In desperation,

I phoned Yorkshire Television, which has a line through to a taxi firm, and within minutes the agony was over.

After that, George Little came to stay with me and protect me, and very kind he was too. But I couldn't settle. Peter came up and we eventually found a house a short distance from the studios.

On screen, *Emmerdale Farm* was going from strength to strength. It began on ITV as a twice-weekly serial to fill in the extra daytime programming hours that had arisen after broadcasting restrictions were dropped by the government. So popular was the serial that it was soon moved from its Monday and Tuesday lunchtime slot to a teatime one and had viewing figures of three million.

The story was moving apace. After Jack's return to Beckindale, the Sugdens turned the farm into a profitable business and took the advice of Henry Wilks, who had made his fortune as a Bradford wool merchant, taken early retirement and bought a large house in the village. They formed a company, Emmerdale Farm Ltd, with Annie, Jack, Joe and Matt joined as directors by Henry. He became a good friend and trusted adviser to Annie, as well

as joint owner of The Woolpack pub, with Amos Brearly.

Little more than a year after the programme started, Jack left for Italy to work on a film version of the best-selling novel he had written, *Field of Tares*. Meanwhile, Annie was able to look forward to the future of the farm and the family, both of which seemed bright.

Daughter Peggy gave birth to twins, Sam and Sally, but tragedy struck when actress Jo Kendall was written out and the character died suddenly of aneurysm, the rupture of a tiny blood vessel in the brain. A year later, the twins were killed in a car accident on a level crossing.

Joe had also experienced unhappiness, marrying Christine Sharp, a Milk Marketing Board inspector, but she was not a Daleswoman and her father had been against the marriage. Eventually, she left Joe and he made it clear that he would not leave Beckindale, so the pair were divorced.

All this meant that on many occasions when acting Annie I wanted to cry, but our director, David Green, said, 'Annie does not cry. She cries all her tears into

the pillow at night. Cry all your tears at rehearsal.' That was hard on me, but it worked. I remember Jean Alexander, who played Hilda Ogden in *Coronation Street*, had the opposite problem. She found it hard to cry and never did so in rehearsals, but let the tears flow when it was called for in the studio.

At the start, *Emmerdale Farm* didn't feel like soap—not in the way that the word is sometimes used as a derogatory term, anyway—because it was so good and there were situations you wouldn't get anywhere else.

The television equivalent of touring in a stage play was filming on location, which was wicked in more ways than one. For the first three years of *Emmerdale Farm*, we filmed outdoor scenes in the village of Arncliffe. The day would begin with bacon-and-egg butties, we would have a coffee at eleven—or soup if it was cold—and then a lovely, three-course lunch, with sandwiches and cakes for tea. No wonder my figure soon lost its shape and became *en bon point*—the French for well rounded.

I remember the bitter cold, when your whole body would go rigid. Thermals, hand warmers and layer upon layer of clothes did

nothing for me. I could never get warm again until I returned home and sank into a deep, hot bath. Even my jaw would freeze and I could hardly speak. After a couple of years, we moved to the village of Esholt for location filming because Arncliffe was too far from the Yorkshire Television studios. Our outdoor scenes are still recorded in Esholt and The Woolpack was really the village's Commercial Inn—but renamed The Woolpack more recently. However, these days I don't do many location shots, due to the onset of old age and arthritis.

One other location I remember well was in the Wharfdale Fells, where two of the cast went down into a cave and Freddie Pyne and Frazer Hines had to rescue them. We stood at the mouth of the cave shivering and drinking soup and had the Fell Cave Rescue Service to help us. A grand crowd of lads they were, too. All of us stayed at the Yorke Arms, Ramsgill. One of the rescue service members brought his guitar and played during the evening, with everyone getting in a request and singing along. The night went on until 3 am and it was magic.

Another beautiful location was the Mill, in a lovely setting beside rushing water. In

the story, Jack had bought it and turned it into a home. If you went behind the Mill, it was like fairyland on a snowy, frosty morning. There was a little lake with trees all around and, covered with frost and snow, it took your breath away. We filmed there in October, when all the leaves on the trees were golden. But we were recording two months ahead of the programme's transmission, so it was all wrong, and the technicians had to go round shaking the leaves off any trees that were in shot!

While filming on location in those days, there was only one caravan in which all cast members could change, which meant that men and women were mixed together. It didn't bother me—after all, there's not much difference between a woman in bra and pants or a bikini. But it did bother Toke Townley, who played my father, Sam Pearson, and he would hide in the wardrobe caravan. He never ate with us either, but sat alone near the door of the canteen. He was very much a loner and would entertain himself for hours and hours playing the flute, although we were also entertained when he played it in the programme, usually to accompany children

who were seen dancing.

Toke, who had spent a lifetime as a character actor in films, usually playing country bumpkins, was a real eccentric and we worked well together. He was one of those who had entered acting late, not turning professional until the age of thirty-two, when he joined the repertory theatre company in Birmingham, although he had previously acted in amateur dramatics while working as a factory clerk.

He was a gift to casting directors and can still be spotted in films turning up on television, such as *The Admirable Crichton, Doctor at Sea, Doctor in Distress, Carry On Admiral* and even a horror picture called *The Scars of Dracula,* which starred Christopher Lee and was Toke's last appearance on the big screen before joining *Emmerdale Farm.*

Unbeknown to me, I used to drive Toke mad, because I would mother him and, if his clothes were untidy, tidy him up. I used to phone his landlady and ask her to send his clothes to be cleaned because they used to get a bit smelly.

Towards the end of his life, Toke began to get a bit tetchy with me and I even felt that he hated me, which I found

devastating. So I wrote to him and said how much I cared for him and respected him, and begged his forgiveness for all my unwitting sins. We were friends again—and thank goodness, for not long afterwards he died suddenly.

I was on holiday at the time and had a call from our producer to go up to Leeds to pay tribute to Toke on *Calendar*, Yorkshire Television's regional news programme. I went straight up, of course, but it was a shattering experience to talk about a beloved friend so soon after his death.

The script was changed, we all picked up the pieces and there we were carrying on as if nothing had happened. But the bottom had dropped out of Annie's world and nothing would ever be the same again. We were a very close-knit company of actors and it was like being in a large family, with everyone caring for everyone else. I didn't go to Toke's funeral because I was working, but Peter went.

Someone else I upset was Al Dixon, an extra often seen drinking in The Woolpack and known only as Walter. It was decided there should be a photograph of Annie with her late husband, Jacob, on the mantelpiece and they chose Al Dixon

to pose for a picture with me. I was absolutely furious because I thought Annie should have a great lion of a man for a husband, not a tiny, weedy thing like he was. I took it out on Al and couldn't bring myself to be nice to him, although he was terribly nice to me. I still couldn't forgive him for daring to be my husband. Sadly, he died during the eighties after suffering a stroke.

Kevin Laffan, who created the programme, and I hit it off right from that first interview, and Peter and I became great friends with Kevin and his wife, Jean. He is the most entertaining of guests—it's hard to get a word in edgeways—but I could listen to him for hours.

Kevin, who was a director of production at the Everyman Theatre in Reading before the programme started, had already enjoyed a London West End stage hit and film with *It's a Two-Feet-Six Inches-Above-the-Ground World*. He was also the writer of successful series for Yorkshire Television, such as the comedies *The Best Pair of Legs in the Business*, starring Reg Varney, and *Beryl's Lot*, and episodes of the dramas *Kate and Justice*. Before going into acting and writing, he had been a farm labourer,

so knew something of the setting for *Emmerdale Farm*.

In the early days, he wrote many of the programme's scripts, but more recently there was a disagreement with the powers that be over the introduction of more sex and violence. So, after thirteen years, he stopped writing for us, which I think is a tragedy because there was often pure magic in his pen. He has an incredible knack of writing a scene about something so trivial or mundane as a piece of string and making a story out of it.

Peter Young, who was wardrobe supervisor at Yorkshire Television, was another friend. He loved to dress me up extravagantly and even chose the outfit I wore for my son's wedding, five years after the programme began, although my husband thought it was over-the-top. But surely it's all right to dress up when you are the bridegroom's mother!

Before they married, Nigel and Rosina had found a house that needed a lot of work done on it and I came home for a seven-week break during the summer of 1977 to look after my darling boy properly, which I hadn't been able to do for years. No sooner had I arrived home than Nigel

announced he was going to camp out at the house, fifteen minutes' drive away, so that he could get on with the rebuilding and the decorating. I was devastated. Now, he had a fiancée and, presumably, didn't need tender, loving care from his mum any more.

He and Rosina came over for the occasional meal, but it wasn't the same. I did insist, though, that he stayed at our house the night before his wedding. The day itself was lovely. I wore my dress, the church looked so pretty, Rosina was radiant and Nigel was his handsome self. Relatives and friends came from all over—including many of the *Emmerdale Farm* cast—and we had a very jolly time.

Lots of photographs were taken, including one great big one with all the guests. Carmel Cryan, wife of the late actor Roy Kinnear, came up to me and said, 'Give me your hymn sheet. You'll be sorry you were holding that when the photos come out.' How nice to have friends who care.

Peter Young's creations continued to make me glamorous off screen in a way that Annie has never been. For a Variety Club of Great Britain lunch at the Queens

Hotel, Leeds, at which my brother Brian was speaking, I wore a large-feathered hat. In his speech, Brian referred to it as a 'meringue', but one newspaper the following day carried the headline 'Annie goes to town on a hat'.

On another occasion, Peter Young took me to a party at the Queens Hotel. He arrived on the dot in a chauffeur-driven white Rolls-Royce with a spray of orchids to pin to my gown and it was a great evening. When the programme's cast met Princess Margaret at a fête, Peter dressed me to kill again and, once more, with a large-feathered hat. It was all rather wasted in the appalling weather we had for the day and, to top the lot, the Princess said she had never seen *Emmerdale Farm*, so Freddie Pyne told her to 'get watching'. I nearly offered to swap hats, because hers was a very boring little number.

Sadly, all good times come to an end and Peter returned to films and design, which was his real vocation. I was delighted to hear he had won an Oscar as a designer and, although I haven't seen him for years, he sometimes phones for a chat and to be cheered up. He was back in Yorkshire a few years ago, to work on Michael Winner's

film version of the Alan Ayckbourn play *A Chorus of Disapproval,* which they filmed in Scarborough, where the playwright had once been director of the town's Theatre in the Round company. Incidentally, Alan was another who started his career as an actor with Donald Wolfit.

Other good friends from *Emmerdale* in those early days were our second producer, Bob Cardona—an American from California—and his wife, Gloria Tors, one of our scriptwriters. In 1976, they asked whether Peter and I would like to holiday with them in Vence, in the south of France. Another scriptwriter, Jeremy Burnham, and his actress wife, Veronica Strong, our stage manager, Prue Haines, and two long-time friends of ours, Marianne and Charles Stewart-Beale, joined us.

We all drove down in convoy, staying a night in Boulogne, then stopping off in Lamastre *en route.* This was an hour off the motorway and the road was all twists and turns with a cliff on one side. I was petrified, but the hotel was lovely when we arrived. The next day, of course, we had to head back for the motorway and the journey seemed endless.

Eventually, we arrived at our villa, only to find it jinxed. Jeremy and Veronica's bed collapsed, Charles sat on a hammock that collapsed, Marianne stood on a chair that collapsed and someone else knocked a picture off the stairs wall. But we rose above it all! Because we were four-and-a-half families, we took it in turns to do the catering. This meant that for two days out of four you spent one shopping and planning and the next cooking. Of course, everyone tried to outdo the previous menu and we had a wonderful time.

By day, we went on the beach, once going to Cannes, where we had a square yard between four people. At night, we would go into the woods, lit by fireflies. We played games on the veranda and cards every evening, with Jeremy being a master card trickster and outwitting us all every time. After three lovely weeks, we travelled home the easy way, putting the cars on the train.

Shortly afterwards, Bob left the programme as its producer and we were all devastated. He had been on it three years and I remember once, when he was also directing the serial, the head of drama, Peter Willes, went into the

control room. I panicked and could do nothing right because he was there. Bob came steaming downstairs, grabbed hold of me—a trembling woman—and said, 'Please do it—just for me.' Of course, I carried on and Peter didn't come near us again until the death in the story of Matt Skilbeck's twins, when he came to the production run and, thankfully, was duly impressed.

On another holiday abroad, I found myself in the same hotel as Frazer Hines. I had arranged to go to Corfu with my friend Anna Dawson, who appeared in many of the Whitehall farces but is probably best known to television viewers from *The Benny Hill Show*. We arrived at the hotel to find Frazer there—and life is never dull with him around. We had a lot of fun and even learned Greek dancing. Oh, my poor knees! I enjoyed many holidays, which is one of the perks of earning good money on a top television programme, but I was always glad to get back to the studios.

It wasn't such a welcome return, though, when I drove my car into a wall and nearly landed in reception. I stepped out of the car to move a cone so that I could park, climbed back in, stretched and hit the

accelerator. I remember thinking in that short space of time, 'Shouldn't be moving. I haven't started yet.' I saw a car ahead of me and pulled the wheel round to go under an archway, but there was no time and I went straight into the wall. I hadn't even had time to 'clunk-click' my seat-belt, so how I didn't go through the windscreen I don't know.

As the car hit the wall, there was a terrific explosion and I thought I was dying. With help, I got out of the car—which was a write-off—and was wheeled to the nurse's office, where I started to turn sleepy. Shirley, the nurse, hit me and said, 'For God's sake, don't go to sleep on me, Sheila.' I had only bruised my legs and hurt my ribs and wanted to go back to work because it was a production day, but the doctor said I must go home. I had been back only ten minutes when the press started calling, wanting to know the story. I was in no state to talk to them, so what they then printed was rubbish.

There were many stories and much laughter about me after that. The cast named a cocktail the Sheila Wallbanger. Then, one day, I heard over the Tannoy, 'Sheila Mercier to reception. No, not that

fast, Sheila!' I laughed it all off. If I hadn't, I would have cried. Inside, I was crying because I had never made a mistake in a car before and it was somewhat unnerving.

One of our producers, Richard Handford, always seemed to get the mucky end of the stick. He was forever having to gather his scriptwriters together and change the storyline or write somebody out for a few episodes because of unforeseen circumstances. Richard must have been in despair sometimes. On his seventieth birthday, Toke Townley celebrated by starting to dance on the table in the Green Room, but the table collapsed and he broke his arm, so a few words had to be added to explain the sling. It was much more serious, of course, when Toke died, Hugh Manning and Ian Sharrock both lost their fathers and I suffered a perforated ulcer.

Away from the studios, my own personal traumas were mounting up. My mother died at the age of eighty-five, having been very hale and hearty, driving her car around everywhere. Suddenly, things started to go wrong and she was confined to the house. I went to see her, and the

doctor arrived and said he wanted her to go to hospital for tests. I knew Mummy would hate this, so I went back to Leeds, contacted a nursing agency and arranged for two nurses to move in. The doctor was furious and told me to cancel the nurses. So off to hospital she went.

One Sunday, we were all together. My sister and I had put make-up on Mummy and rollered her hair so that she looked nice for my brothers to see, but it was obvious that she was very ill. When I had to leave, Brian came out with me and we wept. Then, I dried my tears and went to look in through the window of her room to wave goodbye with a smile, but I knew I would never see her alive again.

We had a very jolly wake, though, just as Mummy would have liked. All her friends came from far and near, and it was a terribly happy day. There was a dense fog, so it was surprising that anyone turned up at all! The next day, we all went back to work, leaving Nora to sort things out. So ended a happy and fulfilled life for Fanny Rix.

At home, we had a new dog, Cassius No 2. Our original Cassius had died in 1963, but we were sitting up in bed

one Saturday morning when I spotted an advertisement in the *Yorkshire Post's* pets column seeking a home for two Labradors called Brutus and Caesar. 'Peter,' I said 'if there's a Brutus and Caesar, there must be a Cassius.' So we decided to find out.

We found a litter at a farm, but they were a bit uncouth and we were used to elegant dogs, so we went a bit further and found a nursing home with a litter of ten—five blonde and five black. We chose a big, black one. In the event, we called him Cassius after Cassius Clay, so there we were again with another Cassius. Would you believe it!?

Cass was a wonderful dog, soft and gentle, fun, wild and adored by everyone. He ate all my antique furniture. If it had knobs on, he chewed it—tables, chairs, walls. He even chewed the wall through to the dining-room from the kitchen, but he gave us his love and devotion for thirteen-and-a-half years. When he had to be put to sleep, unable to move anymore, the vet phoned me at Yorkshire Television's studios and told me there was nothing more he could do for Cassius. It *would* happen on a studio day. I cried non-stop and kept having to go into make-up to

have my eyes fixed. The make-up lady was very sweet and, during the course of the conversation, told me that her husband had died three months earlier. That shut me up. I didn't cry again.

A lot had changed in *Emmerdale Farm* by the end of our first decade. Jean Rogers joined us in 1980 to take over the role of Dolly Skilbeck from Katherine Barker. Dolly had, of course, married widower Matt Skilbeck after arriving in Beckindale to work at The Woolpack on a brewery training scheme.

In the same year as Jean's arrival, an expert piece of casting put Clive Hornby in the role of Annie's son Jack, who had left six years earlier when actor Andrew Burt wanted to return to the theatre. Andrew has, in fact, made some television appearances since then, in *The Voyage of Charles Darwin* and playing Gulliver in the series *Lilliput*, as well as being heard in many commercials.

With Clive's arrival, the character was back and ready for more family friction, although that novel he was supposed to have written and had filmed on the Continent was never mentioned again!

Serials sometimes get criticised for

replacing one actor with another in the same role, particularly when the two look very different. But the casting of Jean and Clive was very clever because they looked so much like their predecessors.

In one storyline, there was a tramp called Trash, played by Leonard Maguire, who fell out of a window backwards and died. Leonard used to be so upset because he had to leave himself unshaven and dirty all the time. He couldn't bear to go into the canteen with the rest of us because he was so unclean.

Many well known faces had come and gone during those first ten years, although no one could have foreseen that those such as Joanne Whalley—who landed a role as a child after appearing in Yorkshire Television's schools programme *How We Used to Live*—would go on to such great success. She was sixteen at the time and played Angela Read, a difficult child who came from a broken home and stayed with the Sugdens for a while through a scheme sponsored by the Church. Joanne also took two parts in *Coronation Street* at about that time, so our popular serials have certainly been the launch pad for some big names.

Other well-known performers in *Emmerdale Farm*'s first ten years included:

*Jenny Hanley, the actress who had presented the children's programme *Magpie* and is the daughter of my great friend Dinah Sheridan, appeared in *Emmerdale Farm* as Briddy Middleton, in charge of some stables.

*Peter Denyer, who played dim-witted Dennis in *Please Sir!*, acted a character called Batty.

*Conrad Phillips, star of ITV's fifties adventure series *William Tell*, arrived as NY Estates managing director Christopher Meadows.

*Gorden Kaye played the village postman for a while, before becoming café owner Rene Artois in the French Resistance comedy *'Allo, 'Allo*.

*Bernard Kay was Robert Sharp, the father of Joe Sugden's wife, Christine.

*Max Wall popped up as dirty old man Arthur Braithwaite, playing quite a few scenes with Toke Townley.

*Frank Middlemass played Basil Arkroyd, before taking over the role of Dan in *The Archers*, the last actor to do so.

*Alison Dowling, who plays Elizabeth Archer in that farming radio serial, was

in *Emmerdale Farm* as Jane Hardcastle and later joined *Crossroads* as Lisa Lancaster. Others later to appear in *Crossroads* were Victor Winding, playing Tad Ryland in *Emmerdale Farm* and garage boss Victor Lee at the motel, and Margaret Stallard, Grace Tolly on the farm and Mrs Babbitt in *Crossroads*.

*Albert Shepherd took the journey in the other direction, having played postman Don Rogers in *Crossroads* and later moving to us as Fred Teaker.

*Fred Feast played Martin, before switching soaps to *Coronation Street* as pot-man Fred Gee.

*George Waring was a chap called Padgett, before becoming Emily Bishop's bigamist second husband in the *Street*.

*Three actors later to become regulars in *Brookside* were also in the programme. Jim Wiggins was Mr Bakewell, before playing stuffy Paul Collins in the Channel Four serial, Bill Dean was Abraham Scarsdale and went on to play grumpy Harry Cross, and Ray Dunbobbin—who is also a scriptwriter—was Dave Duncan, before becoming Harry Cross's friend Ralph Hardwicke.

*Pam St Clement, who played Mrs

Eckersley in *Emmerdale Farm*, later joined EastEnders as Pat Wicks (later Butcher).

*Ken Watson was Phil Fletcher, and went on to play Brian Blair in the Scottish soap *Take the High Road*. He had previously been in *Coronation Street* as Ralph Lancaster.

*Philip Madoc, who will be best remembered in the title role of *The Life and Times of David Lloyd George*, was Paul Pargrave.

*Susan Wooldridge played Margaret Beckett, before starring in that mammoth television success *The Jewel in the Crown*.

*Stephanie Cole, who in recent years has found fame in *Tenko* and alongside Graham Crowden in the comedy series *Waiting for God*, portrayed Mrs Bulstrode.

*Julie Dawn Cole was Pip Coulter.

*Stephanie Turner, who played Ruth Hepton, was later the original star of *Juliet Bravo*.

*William Moore, actor husband of Mollie Sugden, played a character called Jackson.

*James Aubrey, who acted Gavin in that tempestuous drama series *A Bouquet of Barbed Wire*, actually played a priest, the Reverend Bill Jeffries in *Emmerdale Farm*.

*Louise Jameson played a character

called Sharon, before finding fame in *Bergerac* as the Jersey detective's girlfriend.

*Peter Ellis, now playing Chief Supt Brownlow in *The Bill,* had two parts in *Emmerdale Farm,* as Stan and someone called Watson.

*David Fleeshman played Barry Hill and, much later, was to return as the nasty Charlie Aindow.

*Angela Thorne did her famous impression of Margaret Thatcher in the satirical stage play *Anyone for Denis?* after acting Charlotte Verney in *Emmerdale Farm.*

*Tim Healy was a character called Steven before becoming one of the brickies in *Auf Wiedersehen, Pet.*

After Joe Sugden's marriage broke up in the story, he had an affair with Kathy Gimbel, a local farmer's daughter who was played by Polly Hemingway, who later played Gracie Fields on television. The programme was a one-hour special, and Polly was absolutely marvellous. It should have been made into a series.

Joe subsequently fell for Rosemary Kendall, the daughter of a distant relative of Annie's. She stayed at the farm, loved the animals and formed an even greater

attachment to Joe. Rosemary was played by Lesley Manville, who has been seen on television more recently in *Soldier Soldier*. She had a lovely singing voice and played Cinderella at the Grand Theatre in Leeds. She had always seemed such a little, mouselike creature in the programme, so I couldn't believe it when I went to see her on stage and this incredible voice came out.

As you can see, many actors and actresses trooped through the programme during those first ten years. The list is endless. In the early days, though, there were just eight regular cast members, which provided us all with a tremendous amount of work. At the same time, the programme made us all stars and introduced us to a whole new audience because most of us, although having done some television, were from a strong theatre background. We had definitely entered the age of television, where stardom can be thrust upon you whether you like it or not!

9
Fame, the Farm and Annie

Something fame cannot buy is good health, and my memories of *Emmerdale Farm* tend to revolve around operations. I've had a bad back for years and received chiropractic treatment for it. Several years before I started the programme, my right knee became very arthritic. I had injections into the bone and, after the first one, ran up and down the stairs shouting, 'I'm cured! I'm cured!' But it lasted only forty-eight hours, then back came the pain and limitation of movement.

Things went from bad to worse and, eventually, I had the knee operated on by Mr Shea, a brilliant man with a talent for putting people's backs up. But not mine—I loved him. After two months off work, I returned without a bow leg or a limp. Magic!

But my next operation, for something else, was very different. I had flown back from Leeds to our home in Shepperton,

Middlesex, one Friday evening, planning to see my newborn grandson the next afternoon. At 12.15 pm the following day, I suffered the most excruciating pains in my side and couldn't stand up, so I phoned the GP who was on duty. He came out and told me I had constipation. I told him I hadn't, but he gave me a laxative, which I didn't take.

Peter was angry with me because he thought I was making a fuss and told me I shouldn't go to see the baby because obviously I wasn't well enough. I insisted on going and eventually saw the little chap, but couldn't take him in my arms because, once again, I was in agony. I couldn't get my breath and Rosina ran down the ward to get the sister. I was whisked off to casualty and had a perforated ulcer diagnosed. I insisted I didn't have an ulcer, but apparently the pills that I had been taking for arthritis in the other knee and my wrists make holes in your stomach and then kill the pain. Anyway, I was duly operated on and the *Emmerdale Farm* producer and scriptwriters were thrown into chaos again since I had to be written out of umpteen scripts.

That was my second operation. Then,

my other knee collapsed on me and I was in utter agony, so that had to be operated on—again by Mr Shea and again successfully. I won't say success is ever complete. There are times when my knees hurt—going up and down stairs, down slopes, getting up after sitting down—but at least I can walk again. It's only a limited distance, but I can move.

Sometimes I dream that I am running, which I can't do, and it's awful to wake up and find it was only a dream. When I was younger, I ran everywhere, but I know it is something I shall never do again.

After my operation, I appeared on the quiz show *Whose Baby?* with my son, Nigel. It was while we were making this programme at Thames Television's studios in Teddington, Middlesex, that Peter was asked—unbeknown to me, of course—about the prospect of Eamonn Andrews nabbing me with that big red book for *This is Your Life*. I had told Peter that if he was ever asked he should say no, but he said yes and, of course, told me nothing.

So, one day while working on *Emmerdale Farm*, the producer ordered us all out on location for some filming. I blithely

went out to the farm and had a glass of champagne put in my hand, thinking that Yorkshire Television must have come into money, because we had never been offered real champagne before. We were told to sit down and look happy and, the next thing we knew, a yokel was coming round the corner with a horse and cart. 'That's a nice touch,' I thought. Then, the 'yokel' threw off his disguise and there was Eamonn. I nearly died. 'Peter, how could you?' I thought.

I was bundled into a car and taken to a caravan at Yorkshire Television where I couldn't see any of my guests. That wait was the most frightening moment of my life, wondering who would want to come on my *This is Your Life*. Peter was rushed to the house to get something for me to wear and the show began.

First on, of course, was Peter and I gave him one of my rat-face looks, then smiled and he felt better. Next came Nigel, who was white-faced with fear, and my face reflected the agony I knew he was going through. He was followed by Brian, Elspet and my sister, Nora. I wasn't worried for Brian because he was used to this sort of thing, but I was worried about what he

might say, so the look of anxiety never left my face until the family were all sitting down.

The *Emmerdale Farm* cast all came in and sat down, but no one said anything, which surprised me. There were only eleven of us in the cast in those days, compared with a couple of dozen now.

One person I was particularly pleased to see was Christine Russell, a very dear friend and actress whom I had known since 1946, when we went to Germany together in the stage play *Exercise Bowler*. I was always happy in her company but, when we arrived back in Britain, we all went our separate ways.

I didn't meet Christine again until we bumped into her at the Strand underground station once when she wasn't working. I was employed at the Whitehall Theatre by then, so I said, 'Come and see Brian.' Christine became my understudy and she and her husband, 'Slim' (Dennis) Ramsden, have been part of our lives ever since. So it was good to see her again.

Next came my grandson, David, blowing kisses to me on film. He was adorable. Frank Thornton, best known to viewers as Captain Peacock in the comedy series

Are You Being Served? and appearing on stage in London at the time, also sent a filmed message. He had been our leading man in Bridlington all those years ago in rep and we had often acted together.

He and I played husband and wife in *Present Laughter* and, sitting in his dressing-room for *This is Your Life*, Frank was wearing the dressing-gown that he had worn as Garry Essendine in that play. Over the years since, we had met at various parties and kept in touch.

Ronnie Marsh, who was in *Private Lives* with me at Middleton St George during the war and piloted me to be demobbed, came on the show, too. After his wartime job as a squadron leader, he had acted and joined the BBC, later becoming a director, producer and executive producer, before taking charge of serials and series, overseas sales and co-productions. Since retiring, he had gone back to the BBC as a consultant.

Dinah Sheridan was next. She had appeared with me all those years ago in *Sweet Aloes* at Huddersfield Rep when we used to have a star in the cast every week. We kept in touch with Dinah and her daughter Jenny Hanley, who acted Briddy

ANNIE'S SONG
My life & Emmerdale